Life's Wonders

Edited by Donna Samworth

forwardpress

First published in Great Britain in 2008 by:
Forward Press Ltd.
Remus House
Coltsfoot Drive
Peterborough
PE2 9JX
Telephone: 01733 898108
Website: www.forwardpress.co.uk

All Rights Reserved

© Copyright Contributors 2008

SB ISBN 978-1 84602 068 7

Foreword

Although we are a nation of poets we are accused of not reading poetry, or buying poetry books. After many years of listening to the incessant gripes of poetry publishers, I can only assume that the books they publish, in general, are books that most people do not want to read.

Poetry should not be obscure, introverted, and as cryptic as a crossword puzzle: it is the poets' duty to reach out and embrace the world.

The world owes the poet nothing and we should not be expected to dig and delve into a rambling discourse searching for some inner meaning.

The reason we write poetry (and almost all of us do) is because we want to communicate: an ideal; an idea; or a specific feeling. Poetry is as essential in communication, as a letter; a radio; a telephone, and the main criterion for selecting the poems in this anthology is very simple: they communicate.

Contents

Title	Author	Page
Bad Religion	Trevor De Luca	1
At The Gate	Christine Mary Creedon	2
The Invite	Jack Pritchard	3
I See ;)	Anthony Rosato	4
New Beginnings	David Garside	4
The Interview	David Thurlow	5
Catkins	Margaret Pedley	5
A Little Boy Lost But Now Is A Man	Steven Hart	6
The End	Joan Prentice	7
Colour Blind	Irene Reid	8
Ghosts	Susannah Woodland	8
Hold Her Hand	Karen Logan	9
Retribution	Keith Brack	9
A Day In The Life Of Bruce's Spider	Geoffrey Speechly	10
Tying The Knot	Heather D Pickering	11
Masquerade	Shirley Anne Neuville	12
Howling At The Moon	Charlie McInally	13
Fat Little Maggot	Wally	14
The Purpose Of Life	Kenneth David Spencer	15
Beach Walking	Doreen Hampshire	16
Lavender Pillow	Theresa Leahy	16
Actress Attacks A Paparazzo	Richard Birch	17
Violet Should Die	Yousaf Shah	17
The Pleasure Of Living	M P Francis	18
Truffling	Patricia Marland	19
Flower Of My Heart	Violet M Corlett	19
Grace At Thirteen	Olive Bedford	20
Another One	Terry Daley	21
A Baby For You And Me	Michelle Barnes	22
The Inner Me	Kenneth Ryan	22
Blue Yonder	Leean Story	23
The European Constitution Sonnet?	Edmund Saint George Mooney	23
In One Ear Out The Other	Sid 'de' Knees	24
Bouncing Billy	Mabel Dickinson	25
Lady Courage	Catherine Burtle	26
Together Forever	Debra Wilson	27
Thoughts	Alison Morgan	28

True Friendship	Elizabeth Bitshuangu	28
Just A Moment For Me	Tamer Mossud Mamoud Abu Amara	29
Wallflower Surprise	Shireen Markham	29
Wacky Dream	Mary Woolvin	30
Face Me	Elizabeth Price	31
Joy	Joy Saunders	31
Our Dream World	Evelyn Mary Eagle	32
A Poet And A Painter	Ian McCrae	33
Gone	Gemma Slavin	34
Living The Pages	Hilary Jill Robson	35
This Poet Late	Roger Mosedale	36
Ashington (Pit Boots And Pinnies)	Celia Auld	37
A Victim Of Our Time	Lisamarie Ward	37
Man Or Monkey	Jean Paisley	38
Perfect	Jordan Hatch	38
Rhyme And Reason	Ian Morrison	39
Valiant	Lee Connor	39
The Vampire	John Black	40
A Warm Welcome	Tim Jarvis	41
Tourists	Margaret Sanderson	42
Control	E S Segust	43
Home Town Wonderland	Kathleen Potter	44
Free Flyers	Mark Musgrave	44
Surviving My Plight	Graham Connor	45
Untitled	Alan Dryden	45
Meal Planner	Sean Conway	46
A Free Spirit	Barbara Welsby	46
Old Clonmel	Aileen Atcheson	47
My Special Daughter	Vanessa Stevens	47
Freedom	Frank L Ludwig	48
A Place Called Home	L Needs	48
If	Donna Salisbury	49
Road Of Life	S Sanlon	49
The Silent World	Christine Corby	50
Rock Of Ages	Kenneth Lane	50
The Graveyard	Fiona Allison	51
Hollow Dreams	Sue Meredith	51
Angels Alliance	Aron Robinson	52
Life Together	Christine Wallis	53
Refuge	Jane Air	54

Being Betrayed	Karen Marie Jenkins	55
Friends	Joan Hammond	56
Lucky Stars	Susan Carr	56
Flip-Flop, Slap-Slop	Gillian Fisher	57
To Hold You	Maureen Thornton	57
If Only . . .	Emma Higgs	58
Rain	Jack Parker (9)	58
Our England	Carmel Allison	59
Toupee	Peter Lee	59
Searching	Mea Tate	60
Hand In Hand	Maureen Westwood O'Hara	61
2006	Jacqueline Williams	62
Watching You	Helen King	63
Pandora's Box	Annabelle Tipper	64
Emotions	Sylvia Smith	65
Mummy	Adrian King	66
Pandora's Sonnet	Barry Bradshaigh	67
Consuming Means	Elwyn Johnson	68
Night Of The Dragon	Bill Hayles	69
The Day I Saved Your Life	Ian McNamara	70
The Fly Catcher	Christopher Taylor	71
Princess For A Day	Brian Page	72
Kneel	C Hawthorne	73
In The Days Of Me Dad And Mum	Thomas Gallagher (formerly Johnny Lane)	74
Dark Reflections To A Dream	Victorine Lejeune Stubbs	75
The Romans At Ribchester	Margaret B Baguley	76
The Choice Is Yours	Brian Hurll	77
My Hero, My Son	Mum	78
History Repeats Itself	Ellen Spiring	79
September	Thomas Ryland	80
Broken Pieces	Charles Keeble	81
Untitled	Wendy Walker	82
The Beat Of Your Heart	Rod Trott	83
The Sibling	Patty Rogers	84
Sound Senses - Sunset	Josie Lawson	85
The River Of Time	Raylton Dixon	86
Seven Deadly Sins	Mavrinder Singh Dhothar	87
Everything For The Office	Josephine Smith	88
A Holiday In The Baltics	June Melbourn	90
Beloved Peak District	John Field	91

Search	Henrietta Valmore	92
3.33am	Christine Bridson-Jones	93
Dreams Of Childhood	James Tracey-Burner	94
The Toxic Garden	Walter Harris	95
My Love	Leah Vernon	96
A Knight To Reply	Andy Cameron	96
Young Forever	Christian Schou	97
The # Key	Matthew R Worthington	97
Who Does The Cooking In Your House?	Ian Lowery	98
Why Me?	Karen Dennis	99
Ps & Queues	Christopher Melhuish	100
Geordieland	Marion Brown	101
My Brave Little Man	Carol Paxton	102
Life Is A Blackberry	Ann Palmer	103
She	Beth Harmston	104
The Dream Tunnel	Maud Eleanor Hobbs	105
September Rain	Andrew Blakemore	106
Timing	Margaret Ann Wheatley	107
The Calm'r Mind	M Sam Dixon	108
Daisies And Buttercups	Alan Millard	109
Always, Always Do	Daniel White	109
Count Your Blessings	Irene A Dalzell	110
Reflection	Daisy Wells	111
Sadness	Natalie Mallory	112
Live And Let Live	Alan Green	112
Round 100	Helen Crick	113
Hobbies	Lily Wilding	113
Say Goodbye	Sue Godsell	114
My Wonderful Mum	Stephanie Leese	115
Street Singer	Kevin Power	116
Waves Wash Over Me	Neil Renwick	117
Back To The Sea	Kenneth Mood	118
Wildlife	Derek Tanton	119
Talent	Valerie Ovais	120
Wonderment	Susan Mullinger	120
Tribute To North East Coal Miners	C Slater	121
Tears	Deborah Storey	121
Cancer Ward	Elizabeth Ann Farrelly	122
Retirement January 31st 2007	Thelma Jean Crossham Everett	123
Together Again	Rodger Moir	124

Title	Author	Page
Norman	Gary Austin	125
An Inconvenient Spoof	Rob Barratt	126
Learning And Trust	Jim Anderton	127
Everywhere	Pedi Fribence	127
Looking In From Without	Chris Sullivan	128
You And I	Kimberly Harries	128
Questions And Answer	James Thomas Rodbourn	129
Hyper Happy	Kim Davies	129
Jamie Through The Looking Glass	Jamie Caddick	130
Smile	Peter Mahoney	132
Waiting	E Holcombe	132
If I Had A Coin (Or Two)	Tracey McDicken	133
Sir John	David Thomas	133
If	M B Tucker	134
Things In Life	Olivia Griffiths	135
The Answer To Everything	Lynda Hughes	136
Firework Display	Jean McGovern	138
Never May These Gospels Scream	Andrew Wright	139
Reunited	Raymond Gurney	140
A Warden's Life	Olive White	141
The Travelling Tramps Visit Spain	Ernest Hannam	142
An Ode To A Dying Village	Kathy B	143
Quote The Raven	Patrick Mullen	144
Mouse	Christopher Cloarec-Pollard	144
Copy Cat Syndrome	Betty Bukall	145
Wet Day	Barbara Tozer	145
At Seventy-Six	Nabil M Mustapha	146
England	Joana Sam-Avor	148
Senses	Betty Prescott	149
Caged Bird Of Youth	Maryam McKenna	150
If Only . . .	William Stannard	151
Inequities	Des Beirne	152
Sympathetique	Roger N Taber	153
I Won't Stay And Get In Your Way	John Wayre	154
Dad	Joanna Wallfisch	155
The Hard Life	Frederick Lewis	156
Inspiration	Michele Cavannah	157
Dear Tesco	Kerry Moores	158

Title	Author	Page
The Poppy	Yvonne Chapman	159
No One Seems To Care!	Terence Leonard Pilditch	159
Ode On A Toilet Roll	Lauren Hesford	160
Treasured Memories	Dianne Audrey Daniels	161
National Service	William Burkitt	162
I Have To Make A Lie	Marinela Reka	163
Noises In The Night	Amy Owens	164
The Snowman	Wendy Orlando	166
My Flower	Madeline Richardson	166
The Pain	Jonathan Doran	167
Diffuse Your Muse!	G Baker	167
The Party	Gillian Petainek	168
The Silly, Funny, Rascal Clown	Jamie Parkinson	169
Yorkshire Discovery Tour	Ronald Rodger Caseby	170
Summer	Nigel Evans	170
You Are The . . .	Nasheeha Nasrudeen	171
Unstoppable	Joanna Frankwick	171
Words Entwine	Ann Beard	172
The Buzzards	David Green	173
War	Emily Petrolekas	174
Our Meeting Place	Pat Little	174
Maj Waghorn's Statue At Chatham	Robert John Collins	175
Eyes	Jaden Whittall	175
My Beautiful	Gavin Manning	176
A Gift	Deborah Wainman	176
The Pavilion Gardens As Viewed By Prinny	Anne Furley	177
Total Recall On The Mountainside Blasket Islands - Co Kerry, Ireland	Winifred Curran	177
A Special Walk	Francis Allen	178
Gallowgate, Newcastle	Alan C Brown	179
Wishes He Could Turn Back Time Or Even A Page	Stephen Owen	180
The Reluctant Footballer	Alex Branthwaite	181
The Hidden Secrets Of Her Life	Shelley Brace	182
Shells	Anthony Orless	183
Untitled	Claire Patterson	184
Intensive Care	Angela Hobson	186
Dieting In Stages	Frank Harper	187
I Didn't Know	Christopher Thomas	188

Dorothy	Natalie Williams	189
Latisha Faye	Jeff Hobson	190
Freedom	Saffiya Sheikh	191
Barlborough	André Bradley	192
A Subtle Departure	Oliver Barrett	193
The Malvern Hills	Jean Martin-Doyle	194
On Finding Some Old Photographs In The Attic	Sheila Smith	194
Motherhood	Prudence Regan	195
There Comes A Time	Desmond Chapman	195
Our Rebecca	Ella Wright	196
Changing Room	Rachel Mitchell	196
Flower Died	Ray Ryan	197
Spring	Patricia Milnes	197
Cannibal King	Clive Macdonald	198
Bleak Despair	Darren Morley	199
Felixstowe Sunset	Adrian Bullard	200
A Hug's My Drug	Sarabjit Parmar	201
Shadow	Martin Dix	201
Forbidden	Ailsa Keen	202
Didn't We Use To . . . ?	Sharon Grimer	202
Peace	Tony Johnson	203
Blackpool Lights	Terri Brant	203
Just Like Summer Storms	Stuart Adams	204
The Farmer Takes A Life	Margarette Damsell	205
Titled	Francis Page	205
Our Washing Line	Barrie Butterton	206

The Poems

Bad Religion

There is a creature
That stalks the earth
And here's its story
For what it's worth:

This monster was born
In a madman's head
Whose heart was cold
Still beating, yet dead.
He cast his eyes
On all those around
Then his forehead creased
With an awful frown.
'You will all pay
For what you've done
Just wait and see
When God's kingdom comes!'
The people in terror
Fell to their knees;
'God please forgive us!'
Were their anguished pleas.
Thus was it born
This creature of dread
That adorns its altar
With the living dead.
Since then until now
It hunts unbelievers down
And makes them wear
Its cruel, thorny crown.

Now there are few
Who've escaped this fate
Will there be redemption
From this relentless hate?
Well, God only knows
Perhaps it's too late.

Trevor De Luca

At The Gate

Two-faced Janus sits at his gate.
    Behind him - summer flood.
Over his head, a sky of slate
    Before him, fields of mud.
Sinewy arms rise to command
Wild rivers spill over this land.

Himself, a figure gaunt and grim,
    He stirs up storms at sea.
Towering waves gratify him.
    Wind uproots a tree
Though why cast down remains obscure
Across our road to the future.

To lighten our days, no hurry,
    Just sleet or swirling snow.
More flung in another flurry
    Where crested snowdrifts flow.
His farewell to us is frigid
With icicles that hang rigid.

No two-faced Janus at the gate.
    A change in weather? None.
For brighter days we still must wait.
    With him snow should have gone
But our world is left so austere
And yet - look there! Snowdrops appear.

Christine Mary Creedon

The Invite

I had an invitation
From one of tender years
The kind of invitation
That invariably endears
An impromptu invitation
Which thrilled to one extreme
This was an invitation
Of which the older dream,

And so by invitation
I joined a company fair
On a very special occasion
In a setting surely rare
'Twas the local girl guides birthday
Sixty and two, the score
Assembled were a congregation
Mostly Baptist, a hundred or more,

A date extremely special
Listen, look and sing
Trio played sweet music
With a most delightful swing
Yet 'twas not the celebration
That proved beyond compare
But the lovely invitation
From a young one to be there.

Jack Pritchard

I See ;)

Showering you with hugs and kisses
With smiles from a heartbeat this wondrous day
Looking forward soon to greet you
With love in our friendship and snuggles in play
Rubbing noses like Eskimo lovers
Touching hands with dew of the morn
Happiness flows in a dance of the living
Eternally protecting the womb from the thorn
With a soul for a gift when sharing the jewel
It's filled with the essence to give life a lift
The way is much meeker than spending in fuel
Travelling the distance beyond valleys in rift.
Hoping with want in desire for a walk
Over English countryside in arms as we talk
So may this day now be one held forever
As the beginning of time, with time yet to come
And never the sandman shall be spoken so clever
For knowing that our friendship derives the right sum.

Anthony Rosato

New Beginnings

The 21st of December 2007
Was for us a golden day,
The anniversary of fifty years of married life.
We celebrated as is customary on such occasions
Another milestone of our lives together.
But milestones are to be passed
On the journey of life
For the next day is a new beginning.
Indeed, every day is a new beginning
Until our journey's end.
And when that journey ends
And earthly new beginnings cease,
Then we shall have a new beginning
In that land of heavenly peace.

David Garside

The Interview

Here I am in snowy York, there's such an air of gloom,
I'm ready for my interview, prepared to meet my doom.
I go to show my brains, my skill and my brilliant wit,
Alas my confidence drains, for I know I look a twit.
Then I meet the principal, a man with sternish face,
If he's as surly as he looks, I'll never get a place!

He eyes me up, he eyes me down, I don't give a hoot
And then he asks me suddenly, 'Is that your brother's suit?'
I answer him disdainfully with not a hint of sarks,
'This cost me all of fifty quid in dear old Marks and Sparks!'
My mother took my trousers in for my trip to York
In my groin they were too tight, soprano I did talk.

This distressed the principal, he certainly didn't rejoice
To hear a six-foot-six young man who spoke with a woman's voice.
The principal was unconvinced, my gender he did doubt,
And to my utter disbelief, the blighter threw me out!
Oh well that's it, I'm finished now, I'm feeling such a wally,
I'll just have to sink real low and go to Portsmouth Poly!

David Thurlow

Catkins

Last years catkins are still hanging on the tree,
Why are they there, are they waiting for us to see
That the unnecessary clutter of the past
Should be made to last and last?
The catkins will fall and as they do
Our regrets will die as we wait for the new!
Only nature knows why if we stand and stare
That all of our answers will be gathered there.
Our souls are as free as they always were,
Our past lies behind us the story told,
But what of the future waiting to unfold?

Margaret Pedley

A Little Boy Lost But Now Is A Man

There are many things that I would change in my life,
My past is the one thing that has caused me grief.
I lost my way due to a lack of guidance.
I was young, stupid, I tested people's patience.
People made choices, they thought it was best,
A lonely soul put to the test.
I had to deal with life like a man
Just a little boy, a lost dog in the rain.
How can you tell what's for the best
When all that you do is just like a test?
Confused and alone, no one on my side,
Learned to cope and keep it inside.
Mom and Dad, what can I say?
I needed your help, I was losing my way.
Thought I could deal with the stuff I'd been through,
All I ever wanted was guidance from you.
I felt like a tin can, alone in the gutter,
'But it's all in the past,' I heard people mutter.
This is from people, who have a great life,
Jump in *my* shoes, you'll know what it's like!
I've been wearing a mask for about twenty years,
A strong one at that to hide all the tears.
To hide all the feelings that I have inside,
People here I am, your eyes open wide.
'How can he be the way that he is?'
'What the hell went on to cause all of this?'
It's all of the stuff that's been in my head
For all of these years, lying dormant, in wait.

Steven Hart

The End

When you have reached the farthest that you can go
Look back on a life, and still a lot you don't know.
Some questions unanswered, yet you've come so far,
Was it worth all those trials, and worries that mar?
You think of the joys, and adventures you've had,
You think of the happiness, the places you've been,
The people you've met in some of life's schemes
You still are left wondering what life really means.
You know there's a God who made plans for this Earth
You read in the Bible about Jesus, and His holy birth.
Yet for millions of years this Earth's been around,
We know from the dinosaurs and skeletons found.
They now say a comet made of ice whizzed to Earth
Freezing billions of animals in a spontaneous burst.
This brought on the Ice Age, freezing cold with no life,
It must have been peaceful with no people to fight.
Slowly but surely the blessed heat from the sun,
Warmed up this Earth whence new life began.
What must our Maker be wondering about now?
While we poison our planet, soon trees may not grow,
I ask all these questions because I would like to know.
My brain is so limited; there are cells not in use,
My brain, though it's working, plays fast and loose.
Perhaps my Creator is my dream in the sky,
Though He is invisible we can see eye to eye.

Joan Prentice

Colour Blind

The heavens are hidden beneath a black blanket sky
Like a flickering candle, the stars twinkle through
Each breath pinches your nose saying, autumn is close by
And grass crunches under your feet, no longer kissed
                                          by the morning dew.

The tall treetops that seemed to touch a sky of blue
Now have golden leaves falling gently to the ground
The pink and yellow rose petals silently say goodbye too
And the orange summer sun can no longer be found.

In the distance a silhouette of chimneys bellow puffs of grey smoke
Soon the roaming hilltops will be dusted white with snow
Kids with rosy cheeks and toes of blue hurry indoors like other folk
Yes, Jack Frost with coat of crystal is arriving faster than you know.

Asking yourself, 'Why have I never seen this autumn glow before?'
'Why only now do I admire this wonderful, colourful delight?'
I have looked out this bedroom window many times, by the score
Yet I never appreciated this gift from the Lord until I lost my sight.

Now I see by memory what has been there all this time
And I no longer take for granted each and every day
This wonderful world to behold . . . I was colour blind
Will I ever gaze an autumn again? Only the Lord can say.

Irene Reid

Ghosts

In the network of the air
They evolve in smoke and heat.
Impinging my space and looming
Within my body and feet.

Walking through the walls
Ghostly goings on persist,
And when I interact with them
They linger with a spectered kiss.

Susannah Woodland

Hold Her Hand

In her eyes shone her sparkle, her energy and grace
Right now her soul is lost far in another place.
Each day is a step forward, you will slowly understand,
The deep and dark place she is in, she needs you to hold her hand.
Safe hugs, strong arms, a smile, a hug will help her on her way,
Protect her from the hurt and pain and keep her safe each day.
As time goes by in her eyes a twinkle you will see,
A look that will say at last, I have again found me.
Until that day until it's here,
Just keep her warm, keep her near.
A miracle from Heaven, you will feel your beating chest,
A rush of love, a proud moment as her sparkle shines with zest.
Allow her to feel sadness; it will help her heal,
Allow her to feel anger, it makes recovery so real.
I know your heart is breaking to watch her in this pain,
I hope these words will help you to understand how to heal
                                                        her soul again.

Karen Logan

Retribution

It walks in shadows not tainted by light
Where the only comfort is death by the malice of might.
There are no birds that will sing in a place of such dark
Only misery and depravity will be there to leave a mark.
Yet a place does exists in the minds of all men
To extinguish the dark and all it befriends.
So look deep within your mind
Then bring forth the light you will find
For the destroyer of death is the giver of light.

Keith Brack

A Day In The Life Of Bruce's Spider

A spider I, one of the great arachnid race
Who in the wide world's wonders hold my tiny place
My home was made by limited poor creatures whose legs are but
                                                                                             a pair
They think themselves as 'human', and sometimes I despair.

They are so many that for my own defence
I have learnt their language (of which not much makes senses).
One day a battered fugitive from their many tribal wars
Stumbled to the hut, my hearth, bemoaning his lost cause.

You may know - or as I suspect, do not
That websites are our passion, to weave a silken knot
From beam to beam, from roof to floor, this is the spider's art
Subtler, finer, deeper far than the 'works' of their Mozart

He slept, my uninvited guest, upon the heather couch
And slumbered, often snoring, for that I true can vouch
Then came the dawn and I began my web once more to weave
The first threads slipped out gracefully, almost could I believe.

That my masterpiece of art and practicality too
Could finally bear fruit and as a bonus lunchflies two
But it wasn't right, and in a pet I trashed a line or three
Then reconsidered - ah - that's it! - Just add a tiny few.

Until the lucky number came, it's strange, I don't know why
But it almost always works upon the seventh try.
I hear - we spiders keep alert to what the twolegs do
That Bruce (his human name) believed that what arachnids do

Is persist, and try and try again until the answer comes
There's something in this rumour, but by the pricking of my thumbs
(Which I don't have, but I had to make it rhyme)
The truth is that we spiders don't possess a sense of time

We do however love to weave a pretty pattern
For us art is a beauty not a dull and dirty slattern
So our webs are our true glory, and if it takes the rest of time
We'll spin and weave until at last the web's sublime.

Geoffrey Speechly

Tying The Knot

'I feel quite faint,' the bridegroom sighed.
'Hush . . . here she comes - here comes the bride,'
The best man murmured, trying to sound calm,
As the vision in white on her father's arm
Swished down the aisle with the grace of a swan,
With two cute little bridesmaids following on.

The groom turned around to admire his bride;
With a couple more steps she was there at his side.
And, as the assembly of guests fell mute,
He made one last endeavour to straighten his suit,
And wished that he hadn't drunk that double gin
Before leaving home, as it hadn't helped him.

The time had arrived for the service to start
And the bride vowed to love him with all of her heart,
While he promised faithfully never to stray,
And she'd gladly cherish, honour . . . and obey.
As the pair, now wed, strolled back up the aisle,
Their nervousness waned and they started to smile,

Enjoying the moment, in love and elated.
The sun shone outside; the photographer waited.
And, with the formalities all taken care of,
The only thing now that they had to beware of
Was the content of the best man's oration:
A prospect to fear after too much libation!

They needn't have worried for, as it transpired,
The best man stayed sober: a feat they admired.
And everyone said they'd had a great time -
The food was fantastic, and so was the wine.
Then it was time to bid them farewell,
So they said their goodbyes and left the hotel.

On the way to the airport they stole many kisses,
So madly in love were this man and his missus.
And, once on the plane, which was bound for Mauritius,
They ate passion fruit, which they found quite delicious;
And toasted their future as man and wife,
Together, for now . . . and the rest of their lives.

Heather D Pickering

Masquerade

We stood side by side, each with a candle in our hand,
The ceremony over, together we lit the union candle.
The light twinkling on our wedding bands,
Our faces radiant, nothing we couldn't handle.

Careless words spoken in haste
Echo through my mind.
Misunderstanding? What a waste,
Only emptiness left behind.

This union begun with the promise to adore
Has turned into a masquerade.
I've taken my side, you've taken yours,
Like enemies we fight with duelling blades.

In public we are careful to wear our masks,
Assuming that others wouldn't see past this disguise.
Communication becomes a disagreeable task,
Stiff bodies reveal how our relationship has died.

At first it seems pain will not cease,
The tears aren't far away!
All I want is complete release,
Time is the great healer they always say.

I sit here watching the sunset close this day,
So much beauty in the pinks and gold.
Into darkness it all fades away
With it the promise that a new sunrise will unfold!

Shirley Anne Neuville

Howling At The Moon

Alone and aloof from the world again
His well-kept secret hidden deep inside
Awaiting the return of four horsemen
On black-hooded horses he knows they ride

Approaching they come with thunderous hoof
Terror, Frustration, Bewilderment, Fear
He waits beneath star-filled, sky-lighted roof
For those dreaded horsemen as they draw near

Howling at the moon behind the locked door
The book of wisdom was his only hope
Looking through pages as he crossed the floor
Praying those words would cast him a rope

A calmness descended, his fingers froze
Another magic the table did hold
As shivers ran from his head to his toes
He stopped in his tracks as his blood ran cold

Wispy clouds passed by the silvery moon
The horsemen dispatched to return to Hell
The music returned from the Dylan tune
The book gave him strength that he lived to tell.

Charlie McInally

Fat Little Maggot

Fat little maggot was hungry and his face wore a frown
so off he set to get food wriggling all the way until he reached town.

On his travels he met many other travellers walking to and fro
meeting new travellers he did not know.

Had a close shave while on the grass he sat
as he was nearly seen and eaten by a cat
and after all he was a plump little maggot all meaty and fat.

Once again off he set and off he went
no stopping him now, to get food was his intent.

Down the road he travelled for many a mile
ever so hungry and his face void of smile
thinking if himself, *I will reach town in a while*.

He was now beginning to get in a bad mood
as he was dying for some food.

Wriggling along the road all day and all night
thinking, *when I have eaten I will be alright*.

Fat little maggot by now was getting ever so thin
and he had all around his body really floppy skin.

Not to worry, he thought
even though he was getting really distraught.

Then suddenly from a distance he could see the city lights
he knew then that town was now in his sights.

Reached town and made for the fruit store
he knew he was reaching Heaven's door.
But first he had to cross a busy road avoiding traffic carrying its load.

Thin little maggot waited patiently for a traffic gap
one then arrived and he wriggled off across the road to avoid mishap.

He reached near and near to the fruit store
to munch into an apple was all he wanted, that was all.

He raced as fast as he could across the street
to reach the fruit he longed to eat.

He got so near and yet sadly so far
as he was squashed by a fast moving car!

No just kidding, he got there in the end,
now he is a fat little maggot again who is on the mend
and he met another fat little maggot in the apple who is now his girlfriend!

Wally

The Purpose Of Life

Not sure of the source from whence we came
Nor where we're going to,
The only thing for which we know
Is that we exist and are living through
Our patch of time, our allotted stay,
We live our life from day to day.
Not knowing if tomorrow brings
A day of good or evil things.

We don't know why that we are here
Or where we may be going,
We can but try to live life best
To keep our spirits growing.
Go forward each and every day
No matter how slow the pace,
Look back and learn from our mistakes
It is of no disgrace.
Be in the knowledge, other souls have too,
Been through it all, just like you.

Kenneth David Spencer

Beach Walking

The sand is firm
beneath my feet,
and sand is hot
as I feel the heat.
I love to paddle
when the water is warm,
it is so peaceful
and I feel so calm.
No noise is heard
apart from the sea,
no other sound,
just you and me.
I feel your touch
within my reach,
walking hand in hand
along the beach.

Doreen Hampshire

Lavender Pillow

I made one for my grandma
to put beside her bed
so she could smell the lavender
when she laid down her sleepyhead.

It took me quite a while to make
I embroidered it with care,
and now I have it back again,
a memory to share.

Theresa Leahy

Actress Attacks A Paparazzo

Eating an ice cream
Can make you fat so
Fulfil a dream
Attack a paparazzo!

Another paparazzo
Thinks it'd make a good shot
And because that's so
Snaps the creamèd clot!

The actress who made
The attack keeps so slim
Because the Lyons Maid
Is all for him!

Richard Birch

Violet Should Die

Roses bleed red
Violets cry blue
Love is from the heart
But hatred is too

And if the rose should bleed
And these violets should cry
When the rose loses its petals
And the violet should die

The beginning of the end
For change is too late
As I send you this poem
This poem of hate.

Yousaf Shah

The Pleasure Of Living

I stand outside, I feel like a ghost
Watching children play, doing what they like most.
They are creating memories that they will treasure
Memories they will keep forever and ever.
When I was a child I went to this place
I remember my friends and playing kiss chase.
We would squeal and shout, kick a ball about
Play hide-and-seek until our time ran out,
Then all at once the whistle would blow
We would walk hand in hand and in we would go.
Past the place where the teacher would stand,
Suppressing a giggle for talking was banned.
Back to the classroom in a wiggly line
Me and my sweetheart, with her hand in mine.
Where are they now all these friends that I had?
Are they happy or sad, content with their lot
Or are they down and out and no one gives a jot?
It feels very strange standing here like this,
I long for the days when life was bliss.
No cares in the world, no worries, no stress,
Now we live in a world where no one cares less.
We look after ourselves, there's no caring or giving,
Why have we lost the pleasure of living?
Children know how to live life to the full,
They've no time to waste on stuff that is dull.
They enjoy every day in their own carefree way,
Perhaps we should try to be more like them
And then, maybe, our life will be worth living again?

M P Francis

Truffling

A pig with a will and an enormous snout,
Set off at a trot for a forest to rout.
With a sniff then a whiff he routed away,
Contented and eager he'd rout through the day.

His master with trug followed fast on his trail,
He wanted the 'spoils' which he'd offer for sale.
He lived in a hovel - a hut in the wood,
It was draughty and cold and not too much good.

The treasure they sought was a glorious fungus,
A delicious concoction - a tuber 'humungus!'
A food for the rich, its name is a truffle
Found by a pig, a pig with a snuffle.

It all ended happily, who would suppose,
That a pig with a purpose, a ring in his nose
Would enrich a poor man and transform his life
To luxury living and the end of all strife.

Patricia Marland

Flower Of My Heart

Shall I compare you to a summer rose?
You are more lovely I do declare
Than all the months of summer's sunkissed spree
With floras fragrant rainbow flowers fair
Sometimes the great celestial fire shines
And fades the smile of Nature's joyful youth
Time's ploughing the cruel furrows of despair
Where Earth's fast fading beauty tells the truth
But your true beauty, it will never fade
Nor will it dim before my doting eyes
Nor in death fade from life's sweet memory
For tenderest embrace and gentle sighs
As long as life and love binds you and me
The flower of my heart you'll always be.

Violet M Corlett

Grace At Thirteen

You will just long to meet me
When you've studied my CV,
I'm determined to beat the boys
Even climbing up a tree.

I'm athletic and ambitious
In boys' games I surpass,
My aim is the Olympics
As I can run very fast.

My forte is for motocross
Sometimes I finish first,
My dad sells all makes of
Bikes, his shop's about to burst!

My brother says I'm spoilt
As my passion is for clothes,
It may be true or 'tis in my genes
This longing for to pose.

My gran says I should train
My voice as an opera singer,
But Mum says I must study
More, prepared to *pull out my finger!*

My friends are mostly four-legged,
Animals are so easy to please,
I can cope if they are ill
With pets I'm completely at ease.

Now I am thirteen I can think for myself
I'm convinced a job I must find,
To buy my first car - a Ferrari me thinks
As I'm sure I can drive this car blind!

I've not mentioned my name for
A reason, my website I man when I can.
Should you show interest or offer me help
The www will excuse me - if only you are a fan.

Olive Bedford

Another One

Another time, another place
Another date, another face.
  Another song, another tale,
  Another start, another fail.
    Another show, another dance,
    Another go, another chance.
      Another sigh, another walk,
      Another plea, another talk.
        Another task, another job,
        Another smile, another sob.
          Another wrong, another right
          Another love, another fight.
            Another laugh, another cry,
            Another truth, another lie.

Another meal, another dish,
Another thought, another wish.
  Another hour, another day,
  Another stop, another way.
    Another loss, another find,
    Another cross, another kind.
      Another dream, another sleep,
      Another bed, another weep.
        Another look, another kiss,
        Another hit, another miss.
          Another start, another end,
          Another split, another mend.
            Another pill, another drink,
            Another choice, another brink.

Another house, another life,
Another girl, another wife.

Terry Daley

A Baby For You And Me
(Dedicated to Craig Winney)

Why can't people see a baby is for you and me?
It's a bond of love that people share
With an understanding to always be there.
But people show so much despair
They split up and things go wrong
Then they feel to them that child belongs.
Why break a bond that was so strong
For the sake of punishment to linger on?

In my heart I know for sure
Hearts are bitter and so sore
But why break a family even more
By taking the parent out and shutting the door?
Putting the answer in a child's head
That leaves them upset and full of dread.
Thinking it's their fault, the one they adore
Doesn't see them anymore.

Michelle Barnes

The Inner Me

A crumpled tissue on the floor,
with curtains drawn and bolted door.
The outside world's now shut away,
and no one's there with words to say.
We sit in silence all alone,
this shell, this cage we call our home.
Our memories dance with no tune or time,
to loneliness we build a shrine.
We dare not sing, we dare not speak,
our voice is frail, our thoughts are weak.
We cry out loud but no one hears,
we hide our dreams among our fears.
We search our souls for what might be,
we are looking for that inner me.
For when we find what lies within,
we are on the outside looking in.

Kenneth Ryan

Blue Yonder

Another day has come and gone,
Who knows what will come as time goes on.
We wait and wonder for times of joy,
And then the troubles, oh boy, oh boy!

Why oh why do these days come to pass?
Our lives are running far too fast.
We never stop and look around,
To see the glory and beauty abound!

When will we learn to slow down and wait,
For the passing of time and the premise of fate.
We always want to know more,
We will never realise or know the score!

We are only here for a while,
So let's live our lives with grace and style.
There's no need to sit and wonder,
Let's just wait for the big blue yonder!

Leean Story

The European Constitution Sonnet?

All is not well with England today
Brussels has assumed our mantle bright
Taking soon our Queen, sovereign's right?
Donkeys, poodles, cowards do bray
To govern this precious Isle away.
Our helm of greatness given to blight
By New Labour, named in dungs delight.
A pretended countenance, smelly hay
Yet steaming paws for solo, held out
Behind poodles, dungs, tails, empty plate
Spin publishers euros to build stout
Sandcastles of deceit, a smelly state?
All is not well with England we see,
Dung is amused on us all to pee.

Edmund Saint George Mooney

In One Ear Out The Other

Wanna know where I go
when you're bitching at me?
I'm a bird on the wing,
I'm away flying free.
I'm away with the fairies
Beyond the blue skies,
On a paradise planet.
Where everyone flies.

And dances and sings,
About how it's so great,
To be free of life's tallies
Hassles and weight!
So bitch on my honey
Go on, give me grief,
If you think that, that works,
And that's your belief.

And regardless the nodding
You see as reply
That's the flapping of wings
On my inward eye!
Way above mountain ranges
'Neath a glorious sun
Whilst you're stressing and bitching!
I'm away having fun.

Sid 'de' Knees

Bouncing Billy

I'm only a little boy
Without a friend at all,
For I live miles and miles away from town
Or village small.
I wish there was a little lad
To join me in my play
Because I seem to get so sad
Being by myself all day.
Of course I've got lots of toys
One of them's a ball
And I can make so much noise
And no one's cross at all.
My ball it is a real good pal
Now please don't think I'm silly
If I tell you of his name
I call him Bouncing Billy.
I like him to play with best of all
I throw him to the sky
And when he comes down again
Still he will not lie.
I chase him up and down the place
Until I stop to frown
I really must not lose him
Until we move to town.

Mabel Dickinson

Lady Courage

She laughed her way through chemo
Donned a wig when her hair fell out.
The weight dropped off,
New clothes she bought,
Disguising niggling doubt.

'I haven't been this slim for a long time,'
She confessed in the fashion store,
And armed with bolder
And younger garb
Looked better than before.

Gulping tables by the handful
She ate fruits to combat her ills.
And when on the ward,
Played her trusty keyboard
Banished fear with piano skills.

She bore her cross for six whole years
Years interspersed with hospital stays.
On good days she partied,
Finished what she'd started,
'They can't have me yet,' she would say.

I once saw her peer in the looking glass
This lady of beauty and glamour.
Her bruised, sagging skin,
Held the courage within,
Defined by a ghostly grey pallor.

But inside there clung such a driving force
Like a barnacle stuck to a ship.
Her spirit sailed strong,
Hope's candle shone,
As Lady Courage made her final trip.

Catherine Burtle

Together Forever

The sweet aroma of the red juices
A perfect consistency -
Amazing texture,
The hypnotising gloss of each single drop,
Shades of vivid red before his eyes
He looks so peaceful -
So lifeless
With a scarlet blanket, lay there on top.

He senses no fear -
Feels no more pain -
He truly believes he won't see her again.

Knelt beside him, she reaches out,
Running her fingers gently across his cheek -
Moving his matted hair away from his face,
'Why?' she whispers quietly -
As red and blue lights surround his place.

He glances to his side -
His eyes unseeing,
A partial, weak smile appearing.

'I can't live without you!'

Drawing in his final breath
Sirens, the final sound he was hearing.
She stood slowly releasing a sigh -
As paramedics rushed to his side,

'But I never once left you; I've been here since I died.'

Debra Wilson

Thoughts

I sit here all alone thinking,
Thinking,
All I seem to do is think,
My thoughts are taking over me,

Over me,
Drowning me,
All I think about is misery,
Misery
Is taking over me,
Am I crazy?

Crazy, insane, mentally unstable,
Am I able?

Able
To think about anything else but sadness,
Sadness
In the world, in my life,
Is it madness?
Nothing else matters,
My world is in tatters . . .

I sit here all alone, thinking,
Thinking, all I seem to do is think.

Alison Morgan

True Friendship

I am left, you are my right,
In the dark you are my sight.
Two friends on whom I can depend,
True friendship that will never end.
You are there for me and I for you,
Please know my heart is pure and true.
To care and listen when you are sad,
To ease the hurt, erase the bad.
Our bond will survive any test,
Beyond this life and to the next.

Elizabeth Bitshuangu

Just A Moment For Me

Just a moment for me
with you and with me.
I'll be there
in a heavy rain,
in a cloudy sky,
in a windy day.
I'll be there,
in your lovely dreams,
to swim in your eyes,
to fly in your sky,
to sink in your cry
and to play with your tie.
Just a moment for me
with you and with me.

Tamer Mossud Mamoud Abu Amara

Wallflower Surprise

Each spring without fail
Cherry-pink and apple blossom time
The flowering cherry tree
Is such a joy for all to see.

Yellow and reds in profusion
No other shades to avoid confusion
Buddleia, lavender and pinks
Whatever any other thinks
Following April showers
These are my favourite flowers.
Then . . .
Burnt orange velvet appears
More wallflowers after all
To brighten up the garden wall!

Shireen Markham

Wacky Dream

Moonlight beams
Coloured streams
Spangled stars
Chocolate bars
Flashing lights
And motorbikes
Journeys on cars to Mars
Moons with faces
Wacky places
Tears taste like lemon drops
Strawberry, vanilla
Chocolate and candy
All taste good like soda pop
What a wacky place this is
Everywhere just looks out of it
Everyone has all the time in the world
Cars on the moon
Trains that go zoom
People have wings on their backs
Animals talking
Animals walking
It really is so mad
But have I been dreaming
Or do I believe in
Everything that I have seen?
What wondrous things
Cars on the moon
And people all flying with wings.
So sad for me
I've woken up
And now I see
It was only a dream!

Mary Woolvin

Face Me

Stand behind me
Look through my witty eyes.
See what I see,
See what I despise.

Stand to my right,
Watch my back,
Show me guidance, security,
Anything I lack.

Stand to my left,
Be my other half.
Teach me humour,
Show me how to laugh.

Now, face me,
What is left to do?
Kiss me . . .
Kiss me you fool.

Elizabeth Price

Joy

I am bestowed by Heaven above
Perceived in happiness and love.
I'm in your laughter, in good cheer,
In nice surprises I appear!
Reposing in your heart and mind
I surge in pleasures unconfined.
I am cloud nine, I'm mirth, I'm bliss -
The rapture in a loving kiss;
I just drop in without invite
To lavish unprepared delight.
I am the jubilance you reap
Yet sometimes trigger tears to weep
When overwhelmed emotions rise . . .
I touch your heart and flood your eyes.

Joy Saunders

Our Dream World

What a great world, this would be
If all its inhabitants could be free.
Not just humans, animals too,
No longer existing within a zoo.
No more wars, greed or hate,
Everything open to liberal debate.
Knowledge shared, resources spread,
So that everyone had a loaf of bread!
No more poverty, no disease,
Universal language desire to please!
A virtual utopia, living in peace,
A dream world, troubles all cease.
It never could happen; it's only a dream,
But does life have to be as it would seem?
One half in luxury, having it all
While others have nothing of their own to call.
Shouldn't they who have most
Help those who have least?
A wasted meal from the rich
To the hungry, a feast!
Couldn't they with a talent to teach or advise
Show the poor how to help themselves arise?
To create for themselves a new way of life
That could change that burden of lifelong strife?
Would a consortium of the world's best brains
Find a solution to weather, fierce rains?
Global warming and all the issues
That have us all crying into our tissues.
What a wonderful world we would see
If all our leaders could learn to agree.
But human nature is oh so diverse
Imperfection will ever be *our* universe!

Evelyn Mary Eagle

A Poet And A Painter

I'm a poet and a painter
And a teller of tall tales,
But I earn my crust behind a bar
Pouring the finest ales,
Pouring the finest ales,
Pouring the finest ales.

I've got
Brandy for the gentleman,
Beer for the working man,
Gin for the old mother
And wine for the lady fair
And a special smile
For the pretty girl
With ribbons in her hair,
With ribbons in her hair.

And I've got
Racing tips for the gentleman,
A joke for the working man,
A wink for the old mother,
A compliment for the lady fair
And a special smile
For the pretty girl
With ribbons in her hair,
With ribbons in her hair.

I'm a poet and a painter
And collector of wisdom's pearls
But when I go to sleep at night
I dream of the pretty girls,
I dream of the pretty girls,
I dream of the pretty girls.

Ian McCrae

Gone

On a thick grey stone, sits a weeping girl
Wondering what has become of her innocent world.
Where birds once sang and children played,
The happiness seems to have faded away.

Crashes and bangs burn her ears,
A face once shining, now darkened with fear.
Smoke clouding over a sky once blue,
No longer the world that this little girl knew.

What has become of this place in which we live?
Where violence and rage is all we seem to give.
Where broken-hearted women tend to graves of loves lost,
While an evil eye gazes forever down.

On a grey stone, sits a weeping girl
Wearing her mother's gleaming pearls.
The pearls her mother once wore,
The pearls that are now hers, a consequence of war.

Over the horizon she sits and stares,
Of her loss, she seems unawares.
Where she and her brothers once roamed
Waiting for them to return home.

All this, created by Man
No getting away, no matter how fast she ran.
The weeping girl sits, violated by hate,
Alone her world, death her fate.

No light shines to brighten her day,
No one comforts her, no one takes her away.
All she can do is sit and stare
Into the distance at the fiery glare.

A stony face, no trace of a smile,
The little girl has been alone a while.
They said they would return, they never came,
She waited but no one called out her name.

On a grey stone, lies the weeping girl,
Silent, peaceful in her mother's pearls.
No more will she see what man has done,
No longer will she awake to see the sun.

Gemma Slavin

Living The Pages

Almost unnoticed her health began to slide
Until a chest infection bombarded her broadside,
Knocked from her feet, frail legs high into air,
Hospital bedded with constant nursing care.
Later transferred to a residential home
Relinquishing abode she owned, never more to roam.
Gone, her bee freedom
Buzzing to and fro her honeycomb
Another head on life's collision met
Once thought a menacing threat.
Far worse the abject fear than the dreaded deed
When comparing pros and cons above all her needs.
She had clothes, photos and knick-knacks
Recollections in many flashbacks.
Often someone footloose stopped to chat
But, she really missed warm affection of her cat.
Friends and relatives called for chinwag
Sometimes, she, eyeing her handbag
Said, 'Treasures from my whole life in there'
Sadness, happiness, cherished moments thru' years
It is so little to show
After eighty-odd birthdays from embryo.
Nevertheless, the more we live in the past
The less we live in the present
From cobwebs thru' the dust of ages
It has been a wonderful experience living the pages.

Hilary Jill Robson

This Poet Late

The hour imposed upon his aged mind
Imaginings of lanes which wind about in darkened trees,
Old spectres gloat within the freezing steeple breeze
Where distant peels the lonely bell, lost lovers dwell
And angels stir anon in Heaven and Hell.

This poet late did lose the will whose hearth grows cold and dim,
The quill sinks far within its pot, dissatisfied with him
But dioramic turns a star in sky of ink and blot
The casement open to the night gives access to his lot.

Oblivious of the seraph winging far above his desk
His scratch of rhyme was so sublime though wage souteneuresque.
This raven swooped to feed itself is safe now from the gin,
The only hen so dear to him he found in heroin.

The candle flicks erratically, a little spoon, a tin.
A heap is he, his gait now frail and torso oh so thin.
The clock strikes three above the stair upon the wooden hills,
He seeks perchance once more to dream, he has no need of quills.

A Christian sky all brightly lives, the poet eye small quarter gives.
Moonlight beams the dusted room, revealing nought
                                       but shabby gloom,
As slips the poet eye a tear which rises from the cold tiled floor
In splashing coronet of light, his heart a stairwell deep, unsure.

Confounded despair, his crumpled heap, his time is lost, he wants no more
To weep, to scribe or care or cry, thus hard he falls, upon his sleep.

The waiting seraph patient sighs . . .
'Here rest thy head upon my feet and worry not olde friend,
For thou hast entered into life, yea this is not the end.
Forget your lot; come close your eyes,
Come poet, sleep, die safe by me, soon again to rise,
Elsewhere to dwell, we wait for thee, Heaven is thy home.
Beside old man our aged book awaits a fresher poem,
Tribulation tried thee hard, it crushed thy heart's desire,
Be born again in Jesus name for He desires thy pen.
You'll quill the more such verse and wise,
You'll quill the more in paradise.'

Roger Mosedale

Ashington (Pit Boots And Pinnies)

From a scattering of small sporadic farms
A community evolved and turned out audacious
Became the biggest mining village in the world
Men and boys toiled underground, begrimed yet tenacious.

Families washed in tin baths near bright blazing fires
On which women cooked then laboured in floral pinnies
Triumphed over adversity and often onerous situations
Black diamonds ruled their world, everyone was hinnie.

Portland Park Football Ground consistently brimful
Greyhound races, pubs and clubs for liquid stimulation
Regimented rows of smoking chimneys and outside nettys
Racing pigeons, growing leeks for money and recreation.

Colliery bands led parades marching on gala days
Miners' picnics were a time of relaxation
A continuity of tradition proudly maintained
Waving coloured banners unfurled in liberation.

Generations had followed generations with tenacity
Unconquerable kindred spirits of extraordinary resilience
Pit buzzers that hooted like monstrous owls at New Year
Silent, faded into history as fireworks flash in brilliance.

Celia Auld

A Victim Of Our Time

Do you remember the girl you pushed around?
Do you remember when she fell to the ground?
Do you remember why she disappeared?
Do you remember it was *you* who she feared?
Do you remember telling them she wasn't there?
Do you remember telling her you'd never care?
Do you remember threatening her with a knife?
Do you remember the day she took her life?
Do you remember the silence at her grave?
Do you remember the girl you didn't want to save?

Lisamarie Ward

Man Or Monkey

With nuclear fission we are going back
to when we lumbered big and hairy on a forest track,
then our lust for things led us to walk
to where the grass was greener and some monkeys they could talk.
There must have been some bloodshed
over nice sharp tools and chalk,
but, who'd have thought that there would be New York
where now and then a man can use a fork.

Our basic instincts have remained the same
never mind civilization, we have still a lot to tame.
The clash between the monkey and the man,
I wonder who will win and if we can.

Maybe the Garden of Eden was where his days were meant,
to be a life of sun, no secrecy without a life being spent.

The gene we should be looking for is very, very old,
murderers they should have a lot, that's why they are so bold.
Why do our scientists not find this gene,
as, Heaven is when they take it out and make man more serene.

Jean Paisley

Perfect

Perfect is when nothing ever goes wrong
Perfect is fine-tuning the melody of a song
Perfect is writing an essay with all spellings correct
Perfect is faultlessly reading a piece of Shakespeare text.

Perfect is a way of life a phrase no one can use
Perfect cannot describe the future paths we choose
Perfect is putting a smile on somebody's face
Perfect is not sending anything to waste.

Is perfect simply a virtue or an unachievable goal?
Is perfect different in everybody's heart, mind and soul?
Is this poem perfect or does it miss things out?
Is perfect something special? That's for you to learn about!

Jordan Hatch

Rhyme And Reason

Perhaps we should consider, if we do have racist thoughts?
For it says so on our radio and television slots.
Some British folk, it's said, are bad at befriending ethnic brothers
Whilst using wit and humour to make fun of many others.
The Irish, French or Americans, we see as just fair game,
Unless they're of another race then them we dare not name.
And is it not a sad old world when to our kids they teach
That race is more important than justice or free speech?
Political correctness, the religion of today
Decrees what we must do or think and all that we can say.
But that idea's been tried before by others in the past
Then our fathers fought and gave their lives so we'd be free at last.
For is it not through liberty, be we yellow, black or white,
Without the fear of race or creed that things will turn out right?
And throughout every land on Earth because some don't agree,
Can never be a reason to silence folk that are free.
So let us speak with one voice and this truth proclaim out loud,
We care not what your race is but just make Britannia proud.

Ian Morrison

Valiant

More than a friend, you mean the world to me
You brought the light that set me free
Whenever I felt down you walk'd in smiling
Telling stories that are so beguiling
And in-between your humorous jokes
Loving stories about your folks
As I awoke each cold dark morning
Searching for answers between the yawning
Looking for hope in an empty cup
My warm tea gone, so I just give up
But you turn'd up again with more stories
Living your life with ultimate glories
Yes, you are strong with a loving heart
So can you please advise me where to start?

Lee Connor

The Vampire

The rain falls cold upon my soul
The darkest night I own alone
Since my heart turned to stone
Upon that faithful night.

As I watch the sun die in the pale red evening sky
And wait for the moon to rise high and set in the dark night sky
My heart bleeds black as did hers
Upon that faithful night.

Shadows fall upon the ground
There followed by the sound
Of church bells ringing on hallowed ground
As on that faithful night.

As I search the night and wonder
For my need I can't help but ponder
Why I fell for her thunder
Upon that faithful night.

Ah lest the need is fulfilled
And my ponder no longer wonder
For my heart was not black then
Before that faithful night began.

For my needs were different then
I feel for her like many men
I failed to see her real need
Was only the need feed
Upon the faithful night.

For now my heart bleeds black
Blacker than the darkest night
Blacker than the raven in the midnight moonlight.
When life is death and death is life
I am thankful for that faithful night.

John Black

A Warm Welcome

I stood at the very large door
What was inside, I wasn't sure
A wrinkled old lady gave me a book
But her eyes to me didn't lift to look
And most certainly no one spoke
To this nervous-looking bloke.

I thought I'd be welcome in this fold
But I was in the aisle, alone and cold
So I looked around and sat
In a seat, right at the back
But all I got was a glaring stare
That seemed to say, 'That's my place there!'

A stout grumpy man at the front
Told us in a barely audible grunt
To stand up, sit down and kneel
I'm feeling like a performing seal
Then listen to verses, Matthew, chapter two
I did, but what it's about, I haven't a clue.

Then he talked for what seemed like a week
Something about the mild and the meek
Of course I didn't waste the time
I counted the light bulbs all in a line
Then I calculated how much power
To light the room for every hour.

I eventually left by the very same door
The whole event seemed a bit of a bore
The grumpy man uttered but a singular word
'Goodbye,' was the only comment I heard
I asked myself if I should come back
No, next Sunday, I'll stay in my sack.

Tim Jarvis

Tourists

Summer cannot come too soon
For those who flock to South Shields toon
A guest house, somewhere near the coast
With bacon, eggs and crispy toast.

Or some might bring a caravan
And park it where the hell they can -
A football pitch or nature spot
It's free and handy, well, so what!

From nature spot to rubbish heap
In one fast food consumer leap.

Where did our lovely coastline go?
Beneath a pile of flesh on show!
Paunches, flab and spotty backs
Let's pray for rain and pack-a-macs.

They swarm into our pubs and shops
Consuming our beer and fatty pork chops.
Extending our queues at counters to pay
When we're in a hurry, but they've got all day.

When autumn comes, we sigh with relief
'Turrah, come again!' We say through clenched teeth.
Then the clean-up's on to restore South Shields Bay
Till the next onslaught of a bank holiday!

Margaret Sanderson

Control

I pause for a moment and look back in my past,
Some things that I think of cause me to gasp.
Remembering the antics and things as a child,
Some of us got up to when left to run wild.
Through some of the war years no school to be had,
Some didn't even have the firm hand of a dad.
With all of this freedom and no one to check,
We did what we liked, why shouldn't we by heck!
I remember one day while out with my mum,
Along came a policeman, a big burly one.
With no questions asked he gave me a clout,
Then simply remarked, 'He knows what it's about.'
Mum seeing this did not hesitate
And another right-hander I had to take.
Us kids them days would respectfully fear,
The big burly policeman with a face full of cheer.
We were not quite as bad as the vandals today,
The policemen then, could show us the way.
Bright sparks since have changed the law,
The policeman can't act like he did before.
And as they each, patrol their beat,
Have to take kids abuse, sauce and cheek.
These kind of actions now causing alarm
Those clips round my ears did me no harm.

E S Segust

Home Town Wonderland

Slip slapping of tide caressing shingle
Vinegar-drenched chips making lips tingle
Playful wind whistling a sauce tune
Ruffling grass skirts of modest sand dunes.
Surly clouds playing peek-a-boo with sun
Sky-surfing seagulls pounce, fighting for buns.

Sandcastles parading flags and moats
Winner triumphant has boat that floats.
Tommy the Trumpeter is a smarty
Beloved by kids for outdoor parties.
Ducks and swans perform ballet on the lake
To music of small train with squeaky brakes.

Breath escaping with long sighs of delight
He spies a noisy construction site
Topped with a real life Bob the Builder
Directing dumpers, tractors and trailers.
Melody of sights, sounds, smells and sea
His small body wriggles in ecstasy.
Magic Kingdom for a boy of three
Mum smiles too because it's all for free.

Kathleen Potter

Free Flyers

Inner city killings, too many bodies, cannot breathe,
farmer suicide, a loneliness reprieve,
shaping of the menté, by those who govern
poisoning the minds, heads in the oven,
in the asylums they squeal,
a bullet-proof system, like the pope mobile,
but the cracks are showing, as the spirit flies
you can't contain spirit, in a case of lies.

Mark Musgrave

Surviving My Plight

Dreams are born in the corner of my mind
Echoing loudly, fighting to be alive
No sweet tender love like you and I find
It's a miracle to see how I ever survived.
Happy thoughts plague my mind constantly
From when love was felt between our souls
We must face the truth, peace shall never be
Yet we go forth in our plight to be whole.
Minutes tick by, I still dream of you
From one day to the next deep in search and thought
Anything's possible, or so I'm told it's true
Yet still all my thoughts combined equal nought.
I never told you for love was always a game
Where no answers were forged to questions asked.
Waking late at night I call out your name
To prove myself has always been the task.
As the sky turns red I think of you again
So serene at night I'm lost during the day,
I love you dearly, I can't handle the pain
Knowing I don't want you to walk away.

Graham Connor

Untitled

Great literature, the least titillating,
Draws you for a time into its sphere,
Till you reach for the sparkling, scintillating
Play of language to dispel your fear.

That words have substance, this we all can see,
But nothing charms like the free-floating river
Of graceful notes borne onward to the sea,
Instead of leaden weights that prompt a shiver.

So when you look for something to pick up
In idle moments, make it poetry,
That's sweetened with its sugar in its cup
To kiss the palate instantaneously.

Alan Dryden

Meal Planner

Frustration is seeping through my vacant brain
To impress my bronze-haired kitchen goddess
Is all that reminds
I scurry through crowded streets
Passing the temptation of the public house retreats
I resist and desist my devil may care
For I truly believe she will really care
About my well being, physical and mental
So I search the shop for the goddess' kitchen
I hurry back, my food and receipt clutched
In my hand. A welcoming smile form my goddess
She will truly understand
I hope and pray that such a lovely lady like her
I will one day settle down with
And share a haven of culinary pleasures.

Sean Conway

A Free Spirit

I walked along the shore today
'Neath sunny skies from clouds of grey
Tracing footprints in the sand
Leading to a nowhere land

High in the rocks as I passed by
Nesting seagulls caught my eye
Looking out across the sea
Beckoning the waves to me

I stood and watched this scene awhile
Then turned homeward with a smile
Refreshed to start another day
Enjoying freedom whilst I may.

Barbara Welsby

Old Clonmel

I wandered along the bank one night
The River Suir, so noble and bright,
Thinking of those long-gone to rest
Remembering family, friends many of the best.

The water rippled o'er Lady Blessington's Bath,
Poll Traoloch, Duke's Island, the Bleach Yard,
They're all in my path.
Carraig na Soilse, Leath Aidhearch, the Whitning Stream,
They brought back memories as if in a dream.
Does anybody remember the Strand of days of yore?
Bunker's Hell before demolition and destruction moved,
Cascade, The Auk, the Barley Field,
Fiardarraigh, The Locker, they must all yield
To the creed of greed and avarice and money
All sacrificed on the new altar of wealth,
Our old land of honey,
Goodbye old Clonmel.

Aileen Atcheson

My Special Daughter

Through the winding hills of life
Full of disappointments and strife
Sometimes hit by a tornado of despair
Can see no possibility of repair
Lonely and alone without a friend in the world
Freezing and sad in a corner I'm curled
Never hear the telephone go *tring-tring*
The doorbell is silent without a ring.

Vanessa Stevens

Freedom

A moment of compassion
led John, at life's last stage,
to take his little bluebird
out of his little cage.

And at the open window
he held him in his hand,
'For many years you've served me,
as singer and a friend.

But I have been too selfish
and can no longer bear
to see you caged,' he whispered
and threw him in the air.

The bluebird hit the pavement
splashing some passers-by;
caged for so long, he couldn't
remember how to fly.

Frank L Ludwig

A Place Called Home

I'm living in supported accommodation.
At first it frightened me and didn't feel like home
I just wanted a safe place of my own.

But slowly I've learned to like it,
Just work with it and don't fight it.

There are people here night and day
Which makes you feel quite safe,
But the good thing is you've still got some space!

Do I like it here?
Mmm, let's guess,
It's a temporary roof and some friendly faces
No more, no less.

L Needs

If

If I could buy a miracle
It would be laced with love
Angels would be singing
Surrounded by turtle doves

If I could buy a moonbeam
It would be the brightest one
A torch to light the way
Until the rise of sun

If I could buy a rainbow
I'd buy the longest one
And go on a magical adventure
Full of laughter and fun

If I could buy a bag of love
I'd spread it the whole world round
And sow the seeds of gladness
Deeply in the ground.

Donna Salisbury

Road Of Life

When you turn a corner
Which creates another path
Do you choose the easy way
On the ongoing road of life?
Obstacles can lie ahead
Be strong enough to cope
Ignore these little setbacks
That's all you can do.
When you reach your destination
Feel sunshine warm your face
This is when you start to smile
In the ongoing road of life.
No doubt you will get weary
When reaching for your strength
There will be good times and bad
Take each day as you must.

S Sanlon

The Silent World

The little girl runs down the street, a happy little thing,
No one would guess the silent world that she is living in.
Her world is only quietness; she doesn't hear a sound,
Not even the rhythm of her feet a-jumping on the ground.
She never hears the postman knock or the ice cream man come by,
She never hears the radio or the plane up in the sky.
Although she loves her kitten, she never hears him purr,
She likes to play games with him and stroke his silky fur.
She never hears the magic of music being played,
She never hears the birdsong in the leafy glade.
Yet she is still happy in her own quiet way,
She likes to read her books and has many games to play.
Skipping, hopscotch and ball games, snakes and ladders too,
Shopping with her granny and going to the zoo.
Although she doesn't hear the things that give pleasure to you and me,
Her world is still a happy place as anyone can see.
For she brings a smile to everyone wherever she goes,
For God has made her special because He loves her so.

Christine Corby

Rock Of Ages

'You mean these stones?' she moans and shows him five
Found all around their rug under dusk sky.
But, 'No,' he states and shakes his head, 'They're live!
Those Stones on stage, they're our age, don't be shy.'
At once some wondrous noise destroys dull speech
And, wrinkles lit, the signer struts again,
Precision rhythms shake down to the beach,
As, silver-haired, the drummer beats time's bane.
Opaque, the bass supports like chalk cliff shores
Do to the Isle of Wight, all night: Where's youth
But stretched just like the band that ever tours.
Seems this eternity falls short of truth,
'Rock's cleft for me,' she breathes, 'Stones rolled away.'
'Take up your mat and walk,' she hears him say.

Kenneth Lane

The Graveyard

The place which is quieter than a library
The place which most people find a bit scary
The place where the dead are resting
The place where bodies in boxes are rotting

The place families visit in quiet mourning
The place which is full of a sense of longing
The place where the forgotten still lie
The place we'll all go when we die

The nineteenth century stones still covered in moss
The grave still signifies someone has been lost
These stones are overlooked, hidden, forgotten
Under the grass of them the bones are rotten

What about the crypts, who lies in there?
Why is it this what causes the most fear?
Why are we scared of this place and the dead?
In a place of peace why do these thoughts enter one's head?
These questions I've thought about long and hard
But they belong with other mysteries buried in the graveyard.

Fiona Allison

Hollow Dreams

For thirty years it has been my fate
To walk from dusk to dawn,
With every step my heart is darker
As with others lust my soul is torn.

My thoughts wander to another place
As I listen to the gutter talk,
They come, they go, some stay a while
Some just to taunt, or stalk.

Freedom could be mine to choose
Beyond the horizon it gleams,
As ever demanding shackles hold me
Here in my hollow dreams.

Sue Meredith

Angels Alliance

There's a robin in my garden
Behind him there is a tree
There are no apples left on it
He's as unhappy as me
He whispers that there were children
From parents who have careers
Who did not know any better
Falling from his eyes are tears

There is a bee in my garden
Behind him are two white doves
It seems that they have forgotten
About the concept of love
He tells me they were once married
But gave up because they could
They learnt off the human beings
Who just don't act as they should

There is a snail in my garden
Behind him there is no shell
He can't seem to get a mortgage
On his own the system's hell
He tells me he has no shelter
That he may not live too long
It is cold now, it is winter
He has no place that is warm

There's a vixen in my garden
Behind her are her cubs
They tell me they lost their father
Who is always out in pubs
She tells me that he's unfaithful
She's now forced to look elsewhere
It is now what's become natural
Even if it is not fair

There's an angel in my garden
Who tells me I shouldn't change
She says please keep love for certain
Don't let others be your drain
There's an angel in my garden
Who tells me my time will come
Says don't worry, just move forwards
One day you will find the one.

Aron Robinson

Life Together

Thirty-one years, where have they gone?
At sixteen, my heart you won.
Vows we made to make it last,
Now so far in the distant past.

From the start we made our home
Safe and welcome to our firstborn.
First one son and then another,
Both so happy to have each other.

Fun and laughter enjoyed by all,
Watching them grow and occasionally fall.
Childhood memories varied and rich,
Plenty of triumphs and the odd hitch.

Both now grown up and starting out,
The house is empty but I can shout,
'No one can take our memories away.'
And tomorrow is another day.

Those family members we have lost,
Never forgotten, no matter the cost.
Always remembered on special days,
In our thoughts and other ways.

Looking back, reflecting on life,
Still enjoying being husband and wife.
Future memories in the wings,
Looking forward to what life brings.

Christine Wallis

Refuge

A coming-of-winter wind rolls
Spins, bounces and bowls
Down the alley hole trapped
Between the terraces of houses
And old brick sheds of coal
Never reaching any goal

It raps and taps
At my Victorian panes
And shakes and quakes
Not just my glass windows
But the whole house as it blows
I hope and pray for it to quickly pass
For it to swiftly steer and clear
Itself away from here, curling
Back the way it came, hurling

Heavy rain rattles
And splutters
Down my drainpipe gutters
Or impatiently splashes
Down outside walls
In great leaping waterfalls
Meeting with the rising damp
As it upward crawls

Spiders seek safety
In my bathroom corners
Which they grace
With their home-made webs of lace
And as I brush my hair
Or wash my face
I look up and there
From their lair
Back at me they stare

Slugs leave silver slivers
Across my indoor mats
And moths hopelessly catch
Themselves inside my curtain nettings
With only a slim betting chance
Of getting out for one final dance

And a neighbour's cat strolls
Over for a petting
To roll up for a nap
On my lap with a purring tone

All seek refuge inside my home
Making it their own.

Jane Air

Being Betrayed

Unaware the ice was thin
Thinking respect would save
Me from falling in
But the deception and lies
Led to a cruel surprise
Nuking my trust
In a moment of lust

Both relationships shattered
I guess my feelings
Have never mattered
Precious moments now seem wasted
Contrasted against desire tasted
Not even affection
Coaxed a confession

Heard from someone else instead
I should have known then
That my ideals were dead
But even now, months later
I still feel like the traitor
Guilty of the crime
Of betraying myself

Karen Marie Jenkins

Friends

She died, the cancer swiftly winning,
As quietly at peace she slipped away.
The sadness, not for her departing,
But for the wasted time each day
When kith and kin, were oh so busy
Not finding time with her to share.
Her quiet words as she lay dying
Such sadness showed, to neighbours there,
'How well we've got to know each other,
As the last hours with me you keep.'

Her peaceful resignation, was
A lesson learned, profound and deep,
To seek out quiet or lonely folk
And give them time before goodbye,
Means sorrow may be turned to gladness,
When our turn comes to slip away.
To know that we have shown to others
A friend, just when the call is heard
Tomorrow always is too late,
Today's compassion is our reward.

Joan Hammond

Lucky Stars

My stars were so auspicious,
'Good fortune shines on fishes'
That I went off to the bingo
To where the folk who win go.

I shouted house on 43
So did someone near to me,
and further down another three
shouted out just like me.

A £5 share I took home.
'Rubbish stars,' I began to moan,
till my partner reminded me,
'You're not the only fish in the sea!'

Susan Carr

Flip-Flop, Slap-Slop

Plastic foam shoes shield my feet
against all those painful pebbles
flung up to steps and yacht runway.
Those things and a jolly sunray
skirt, say I'm a routine-rebel,

in the merry throes of beach-flu.
I see someone in a striped dress -
She looks like a deckchair, getting
up, and walking from the wetting
shingle, or it will look a mess.

Frisbee, once a beach-bum's game
is challenging volleyball;
as there is no net or poles
or a dibber, to make holes
so the thing will stand at all!
Plastic pan-lids stake their claim.

Gillian Fisher

To Hold You

To hold you
To know you
Brings refreshing
Like the morning dew.
As the dawn
Awakes anew.
To cherish deep within
Blessings begin.
To feel gentleness,
To embrace,
Feeling secure and safe.
These are treasures
They are stored
As the dawn's
Golden rays pour.

Maureen Thornton

If Only . . .

The background noise
The salty air
The breaking waves
The sand in my hair

Scared, alone
Fear, dread
All these feelings
Filling my head

Wishing, praying
The end is near
The wetness of my face
From my tear

I wake
I scream
I wish
If only it was just a dream.

Emma Higgs

Rain

If you like to ride your bike
Get on it and take a hike
Go down the lane
And hope it will never rain again
If it does
Then you'll get the blame
For being wet in the rain.

Jack Parker (9)

Our England

Do people ever stop to think
How lucky that they are
Living in this country
Which excels most things by far?
No hurricanes, tornadoes,
No real drought or floods.
Folk may moan at the climate
But, truthfully, it is good.
There is no greater land elsewhere
Than England, especially in spring.
The summers are just hot enough
And autumn has a sting.
The winters are not bad at all
Compared with other lands,
We've all the water that we need
And lots of food on hand.
So just give these things a thought
Every now and then and thank the Lord
That you were born a lucky Englishman.

Carmel Allison

Toupee

A bald headed man from Leeds
On his head did plant grass seeds.
But he felt a great shock,
As he went to take stock,
And found he was covered in weeds.

Peter Lee

Searching

Steadfast in my identity
Never doubting my history or name
Not sure where the insecurity crept in
Whether by snail mail or express train!

It maybe that I am just growing up
And need a hobby or two
Or possibly I've just lost the plot
And perhaps should get a grip - boohoo!

I never felt the need before
To dig into the past
It surely needs to be uncovered though
To fill the gaps and for me to last!

A bumpy ride it may be
But a worthwhile one I am sure
I hope that I can last the distance
And find what I am looking for.

My search is never-ending
I am learning more and more each day
My life already has meaning
'What if I called the search off?' I hear you say.

Mea Tate

Hand In Hand

Alone, here with red roses
I sit sadly by your grave
Such peace in this silence
Your soul I must save.

Private memories flood over me
Like clouds in a dark windy sky
Their rain gently falls, like my tears
My broken heart is now set to fly.

Understanding is so painfully hard
Wild thoughts still dance to and fro
Our love, a monument to society
My true love, why oh why did you go?

No one could ever match your soul
I must retain it just for me alone
An empty cold world now awaits me
As I sit tearfully, so very much alone.

As a century successively passes by
Our monument, still very surely stands
By then, long-lost in God's eternity
We gently stroll, at last hand in hand.

Maureen Westwood O'Hara

2006

2006 was a horrible year for me, I was glad to see it end.
2007 will be heaven compared to 2006 I hope,
I felt like my life was going down a very slippery slope.
In January I felt so ill I didn't know what to do.
In February I was getting there I went away on holiday.
In March, it was OK, Gary would come and spend the day.
In April, Claire left me so I had to find someone else to do my care.
In May, mine and Gary's relationship was no more, I wasn't sure
                                        if I could take it anymore.
In June I got my voluntary job so I thought my bad luck
                                        would end soon.
In July the learning centre which I attended, closed its doors for good,
                                        which I never thought it should.
In August I went away with PHAB so Mum left Dad home alone.
In September I can't remember if anything happened.
In November I went to a wedding but apart from that I didn't know
                                        where I was heading.
In December I was so busy I made myself dizzy.

Jacqueline Williams

Watching You

I hear you coming out of pubs I hear you in the square
I always stay well out of sight so no one knows I'm there

I sometimes see you in a group and sometimes on your own
You might be walking quietly or talking on the phone

Occasionally your footsteps stagger over towards me
Which makes me feel quite nervous as I don't want you to see

Sometimes I hear you arguing and sometimes there's a fight
The sound of shattered glass and voices screaming through the night

But other times you're happy if your football team has won
A crowd of you are singing and are out to have some fun

I sometimes see you with a girl someone you're taking home
Your arm around her shoulder making sure she's not alone

Perhaps by now you're wondering exactly who I am
Or are you just so self absorbed that you don't give a damn

I'm in the corner over here inside a shop doorway
I hide inside my cardboard box and watch you every day

Helen King

Pandora's Box

I found an old chest of treasures,
Reminding me of childhood pleasures.
As I pulled out each item one by one,
I remembered days filled with fun.

I saw a familiar face, now a little threadbare,
That of my very first teddy bear;
Notebooks with a well-known childish scrawl,
A skipping rope and a colourful ball.

Photos bringing back dormant memories
Sent me into a string of reveries;
Posters which used to hang on my door,
Countless knick-knacks and collections galore.

Badges, erasers, pens and pencils,
Colouring books, stickers and stencils,
Ballet shoes with ties of pink ribbons,
Dolls and cuddly toy dogs and gibbons.

Books whose tales made me dream and smile,
Marbles which were all the rage for quite a while.
I miss those carefree days now and again,
Because life seemed so much simpler then.

Annabelle Tipper

Emotions

The deepest of emotions sent
When birth has come and life is spent
Our feelings desperate to arise
They struggle deep within our eyes

The movie sad, the problem there
We do not always wish to share
The news is bad, the goal achieved
And if we cry, so much relieved

But do we want the world to know
And should we let our feelings go
Pure raw emotions taking hold
We let it out, do we feel bold.

Whichever way our heart desires
To keep within may fuel the fires
Release and feel a problem shared
Emotions tricky never dared!

Whatever makes the heart feel glad
Whichever way, we are not mad
Just humans feeling normal things
Which deep emotions and all that brings.

Sylvia Smith

Mummy

She holds my hand to cross the road, puts clean socks upon my feet
And kisses bruises better, cooks my favourite foods to eat.
She reads me bedtime stories tucks me in secure and tight
And sometimes sings me lullabies to ward off any fright.

She cooks my daddy's dinner when he comes home at night,
After washing, drying, ironing she keeps us free from plight.
She cleans my brother's bedroom cos he really is a slob,
Does all of this and still holds down a taxing part-time job.

She looks after old people, nine till three most every day,
Has to feed and clean and dress them to earn her modest pay.
She does their hair and talks to them and tries to keep them happy,
Then rushes home to meet me there, her precious little chappie.

She's not been very well of late, in fact, been rather bad,
But she's fighting hard, improving well, supported by my dad.
She had a heart attack last year and nearly went to Heaven,
But Mummy, you can't leave me yet, I'm only thirty-seven!

Adrian King

Pandora's Sonnet
(Dedicated to Mrs T Goldberg & Alber)

When I do use the hours that turn the clock,
To make love's treasure mine desires contend,
To key Pandora's chest by hearts unlock,
And rage the winds that bring love's cloudy wend,
So my de-barc now storms upon time's moat
As seconds sweep to 'ours and minutes shore
So sequent time directs my troubles boat
To harbour's rest from tempest loves abhor
Oh now becalmed in doldrums loving blight
Where here love's sentence jails my heart's display?
Shall I then see the path of this incite
To turn the lock that keys love's motions way?
So never was true love or its desire
More wound in argument or truth's sweet liar?

Barry Bradshaigh

Consuming Means

This is the land of our forebears
This is the land of our birth.
This is the inheritance they bequeathed to us
Though intestate, Mother Earth.

When the dawn lifts night's cloak from the day
It reveals the greensward pleasantry of our way.
But will our consuming means their bequest derange,
With a resulting trauma of climatic change?
Will the Gulf Stream temperature mark the gauge
To show a coldness bringing another Ice Age?
Or when heat has constance beneath a broiling sun,
Will the four seasons then no differently run?
Shall we see that greensward turn to brown
Usurped by the dealings of a gasoline town?
Shall the animals of the once verdant field
Lie sickening at the fallow pasture of nature's yield?
Flowers once kissed by the morning's dew
From abundant mass turn to pitiful few?
Raindrops that down to our rivers sped
Seek no further lodgement in that bed?
And trees in leafy conversion never bring
Awesome wonderment to autumn and to spring?
Beyond the melting ice cap will tsunami rage
With tempest and tornado to fill the obituary page?
Shall no bird sing its lyrical summer song
To be carried upon the air where it does belong?
When dusk cloaks the day into night
Shall then tomorrow never venture a pastoral sight?

Though we be only nanoseconds
In the hourglass of all time,
Our trust is to hold Earth's rhythm
In a constancy with nature's rhyme.

Elwyn Johnson

Night Of The Dragon

Two thousand years the Firedrake slept
The fear of his name went from men's heart
In ignorance they laughed, played and wept.
But the darkness grew like a creeping mire,
Unnoticed it surrounded all of mankind,
Who soon would have a baptism of fire,
They may have been forewarned but they were blind,
Eyes focussed only on their heart's desire.
Then suddenly the rock was split asunder
And the dragon awoke and spread his wings.
The people shocked, stared on in wonder
Not realising what disaster the worm brings.
But three knights who had waited for this day
Mounted their steeds as the beast flew
With suits of bright steel and bodies of clay
Their shields bore their names, Christian, Muslim and Jew.
The dragon, breathing fire descended on the knights
With lances raised they rode side by side.
Their armour dancing with heavenly lights
They thundered onward to the riverside.
The Firedrake realised to his dismay
That all God's children were now unified.
He thought he had split them on that far off day
When he nailed God to a tree and He had died!
But the family divided had now been made whole
One father, God, three mother churches reforged.
Their three holy lances piercing its black soul,
Its steaming lifeblood as finally disgorged.
The knights of God, Christian, Muslim and Jew
Are no fairy tale, they are me and they're you!

Bill Hayles

The Day I Saved Your Life

In the city where danger looms
Killing machines and toxic fumes,
Cat-like screams in the hospital rooms,
    The day I saved your life!

Your meeting with death nearly occurred
As you crossed the street where no one would dare.
Flashing sirens silently impaired,
    The day I saved your life!

A week of nightmarish flashbacks, of the moment of infiltration,
A month of counting sheep on electrical ventilation.
A year of sluggish, painful rehabilitation,
    The day I saved your life!

My visitors lengthen my time to recover,
When they come to talk amongst each other.
I thought that I became your brother,
    The day I saved your life!

My injuries still make the doctors whince,
That polished bonnet still holds my prints.
Nothing has ever been the same since
    The day I saved your life!

Ian McNamara

The Fly Catcher

I read an advertisement for a new concept in catching flies,
it's the latest in technology; it may even win a prize.
There's no chemicals involved, spray cans, fluorescent lights,
no batteries are required, you can use it day or night.
So I posted off a cheque to the Acme Gadget Co
although I thought it quite peculiar, their address was in Kosovo.
A package arrived soon after and I opened up the lid,
a note said, 'Made in China' by a company called 'El Cid'.
The box contained two lengths of wood; one marked A
and one marked B
a short note with instructions and a twelve month guarantee.

Instructions:

Take the length of wood marked A and place it on the floor,
Then take the length of wood marked B and hide behind the door.
Wait for a fly to come along and settle on part A
Then take part B and whack it . . .
You've caught a fly, *hooray!*

Christopher Taylor

Princess For A Day

An off-the-shoulder wedding dress
Princess for a day
Long veil and tiara
Sequence from a play

A role but one of many
She'll play throughout her life
A mother and a worker
And a loving wife

Today is something special
An audience is allowed
Who bring gifts for the loving couple
One big happy crowd

The atmosphere is a happy one
With music, food and drink
When everyone enjoys themselves
Some too much I think!

The night is drawing on now
The crowd leaves, one by one
They're shaking hands and smiling
All have had their fun

The princess will be changing
Playing a new part
Whatever part she's playing
She'll play it from the heart.

Brian Page

Kneel

Her hair falls down
As she kneels
Hands clenched together
I know how she feels.

The sense of loss
The sense of pain.
That sense of loneliness
All over again.

Like rain her tears fall,
Like hail they hit the floor.
With a knife he cut her heart,
With no sound he ripped it apart.

And now he leaves her there
Stranded, doesn't he care?
A broken heart,
A tainted soul.

No longer will her tears fall down
Her face is twisted in a bitter frown.
She loved his heart,
She loved his soul,
He used her body to make himself whole.

C Hawthorne

In The Days Of Me Dad And Mum
(Dedicated to my mother and father)

If music be the food of love
And if our God is up above,
Then why are all these troubles here
Upon this Earth both far and near?
For every time we hear the news
And all those politicians' views
It's crime and trouble everywhere,
It's in your eyes; it's in your hair,
It's in your town and in your street
Yet years ago things were so sweet.
We used to leave our doors unlocked
While we were going to the shops.
And talk in there an hour or more
Then talk outside them even more.
Our neighbours were our aunties too,
And in the backyard was our loo.
We had no carpet on the floor,
No hot running water, yes, we were poor.
But I'll tell you we were happy then
And I wish those days would come again.
I know they won't but I live in hope,
I suppose you think I'm just a dope.
But my mam and dad were young and strong,
Now they're gone and it won't be long
Before I join them in the sky
And I bid this world of ours goodbye.
It's a lovely world but it's badly run,
It was better in the days of me Dad and Mum.

Thomas Gallagher (formerly Johnny Lane)

Dark Reflections To A Dream

From tropical groves of spice
To the paddy fields of rice
Passing by the lotus stream
I will bring you, a glint of dew
A nice, little lovely dream

Your face on the canvas of reflection
Revealing the product of insurrection
An emotional labyrinth, what the way to take?
All endeavours lead to love or hate

Calm yourself, shut your weary eyes
The red and wild fireflies
Dance through the fairy green
I will bring you the recipe of the supreme
For a nice, little lovely dream

Images of the past mirror disgrace
Heartstrings have loosened and are just unlaced
How to find the strength from within
To save your soul for a salvation of sin

Don't worry, just close your eyes, good night
In sparkling golden light
The stars around you gleam
On you I pass with a soft caress
For a nice, little lovely dream.

Victorine Lejeune Stubbs

The Romans At Ribchester

The Romans are coming to Ribchester
In all their grand array.
The Second Legion Augusta
Will give their fine display.
With catapults they fire stones
Low down against a net
As if they faced an enemy
Who'd not been conquered yet.

They bring all sorts of shields and swords
And their armour is so fine
When they show how much they carry
When marching in a line.

The Roman ladies come as well
And some whose slaves are they,
They talk about how they are dressed
And how they spend their day.

Ribchester was a Roman fort called Bremetennacum
And parts of it were buried
For many years to come.
'Twas by the river Ribble
Now visitors can see
Remains of it that were dug out
For all posterity.
And in the fine museum here
Are artefacts they found
Brooches and Roman pottery
When digging in the ground.
For ten years now the Romans come
To do their fine display,
So come along and see them
If you're travelling down this way.

Margaret B Baguley

The Choice Is Yours

Capital cities are all very well
But they're noisy, bustling and sometimes smell.
Despite the crowds they are lonely places,
Big shops, traffic and foreign faces.
Probably the loneliest streets on Earth,
Faceless people and not much mirth.
Roaring traffic, horns and buses,
Rubbish strewn and everyone rushes.

The rolling hills are a very different choice,
The birds all sing with familiar voice.
Views for miles, peace on Earth,
Solitary trees with enormous girth.
Alone, but not lonely, so much to embrace,
Smells of harvest, by God's good grace.
Silence is golden, the busy sky blue,
Quiet contentment for me and you.

The world's your oyster,
The choice there for all.
Go where you're happy,
Whatever the call.

The call may be city, office is there,
Difficult location, but family needs care.
Earning big money, important role,
It may not last, but much better than dole.

If country life draws you, then you have that choice
Live in a valley where you hear your voice.
Life seems much slower, more peace and calm,
Work longer hours when you're down on the farm.

Brian Hurll

My Hero, My Son

You grew up in a family that thought the world of you,
You idolised your granddad, he was a 'dad' to you.
But then when you were nine years old, your precious 'dad' just died,
There was no way of knowing and no way to say goodbye.
But deep inside your grieving soul, a deeper pain had grown,
To find the man who gave you life, a man you'd never known.
And, so as not to hurt me, you trod this lonely road,
Your quest to find the missing piece that may make your life whole.
You hired a solicitor; you told him all you could,
The Red Cross was the next step, but all came to no good.
You didn't have the information other kids would have,
You didn't have the background knowledge about your real dad.
The pain you must have gone through, how come I never knew?
How come I never realised what you were going through?
How could a mum who loved her child not see his heart was broken?
While yearning for that missing link with every word that's spoken.
Through my misguided selfishness, I thought I'd be enough,
I really hadn't given thought that life for you was tough.
But then when *you* became a dad, you opened up to me,
And told me all that you had done to find your family.
We searched together, you and I and then we had success,
We contacted a relative who knew your dad's address.
She promised she'd get back in touch within a week or so,
But sadly, this, she never did, and now we still don't know.
We heard your dad had moved away, the gap is wider now,
How can I help to make things right? I really don't know how.
So starting off again along this well-trod path we took,
We hope someone will search their souls and take a second look.
When maybe then a simple call will just end all the pain,
The empty space within your heart will be complete again.
With no desire for angry words, or recriminations,
I know you want to meet your dad and all of his relations.
You have a right to know your past and also know the man.
He helped create who you are now from when your life began.
Maybe he'll never know how much you're needed and admired,
He's missing out on all your goals and the children you have sired.

Maybe he'll never see the man that *you* have now become,
My *son,* my *friend*, my *hero,* all rolled into one.
If I was given just one wish, you know what it would be,
That you could introduce *your* kids to *their* lost family.

Mum

History Repeats Itself

Israel, Iraq and Palestine
All three must look back in time.
Peace there is none that is plain
For the majority in those lands,
History repeats itself again.
Various religions, they are very similar,
Christianity, all so familiar.

People in disbelief, searching for basic rights,
Manmade law produces ignorance and fright.
Closed jaws, the 'freedom of speech' has gone,
Poverty, violence and revenge have won.
Slavery in the nowadays, raised eyes look to Heaven,
Yes, it still exists in 2007.

Will reports always be in a book on the shelf?
If you can read, history repeats itself.
Modern technology retains the horror,
Black, white and coloured, live a 'human kind' of terror.
Hopelessness in the lives of many,
Motivation to fight is waning, there isn't any.

What happened to 'The way, Truth and Light'?
Of equality for all, man has lost sight.
To abolish world slavery, will take like for like
The unity of all nations with the courage to strike.
To strike a blow for freedom, stand up and be proud
To open free mouths, to shout out aloud.

Ellen Spiring

September
(Verses written on a Hebridean Island)

September brought me to the light of day;
September held each turn that set my way:
It stamped the work that early marked my name
Among my peers, and lent a modest fame;
It gave us fleeting years of you to share -
Then brought the grief that I alone must bear.

September joined our paths on Gimmer Fell;
The next September rang our wedding bell;
And then, the gods of fate still pleased to smile,
A new September led us to the isle
Where, resting many summers on its soil,
We said we'd make our home when done with toil.

Then what it gave, September snatched away.
Its jeering sun made parody of day
And mocked our house: a hollow pile of stone,
A dwelling now where once had been a home.

A year I lingered in our market town.
The house grew chill, your garden overgrown.
I sold, I packed, and to our island came,
And here in troubled peace I shall remain.
Though never home - nor ever now can be -
This island, long a friend, will shelter me.

And here I'll sit atop its lonely hills,
Renounce the world and leave it to its ills,
And watch the bird that on the currents plays -
And in the sea and sky, see dearest days
That, though they're washed in pain, I shall remember;
And here I shall await my last September.

Thomas Ryland

Broken Pieces

Why or how would be hard to tell
When the piece fell off it wasn't noticed at first
From an outward appearance you'd say he was well
But from that day on his life would be cursed

It wasn't a physical blow that tilted his axis
As his gentleness left him and deserted its post
His friends now spoke softly as they noticed odd practice
Catch his eye and see the alarm as one seen a ghost

Lost now all his warmth it has melted away
Replaced by the Hyde we all carry inside
No more joy, laugher and song as in earlier days
His sweetness suppressed for what was left we all cried

Life's journey and trials had taken their toll
Wore away at foundations he based his life on
The shell that remained though outwardly whole
Inside just had memories his future has gone

Shadows now lingered keeps looking behind
Nothing in front of him it's as if he's unwound
Just retreated to that monastery deep in his mind
Now hidden from view, will he ever be found?

Season's cycle has passed and time's glue has reset
Broken pieces reassembled he's back amongst us again
Dear friend how we missed you and carry this regret
Why we let you take that journey into misery and pain.

Charles Keeble

Untitled

What is this life we are living?
People taking and never giving.
Perhaps it comes from in the home
When kids are left just to roam.

Families around a table would sit
To enjoy a meal and chat a bit.
But now it's all on laps in front of TV
Or paying games, else watching a DVD.

Do you think we never got to talk,
Take a drive or go for a walk?
But mobile phones and computer screens
Way back then were never seen.

Nowadays we all do less
And then put things down to being overstressed.
But if we got up off our behinds
I'm sure more energy we could find.
To wake up fresh at the start of a day
Not moan and groan your life away.
Every day should be ecstatic,
Just tell yourself that you're terrific!

Wendy Walker

The Beat Of Your Heart

Is your heart still beating
To the rhythm of life?
Is your life still dancing
To the beat of your heart?
If it is then good,
You've found the key,
You've found a way
To set you free.
You've found the spirit
And the soul
The glinting seed
Of rock 'n' roll.
The sweet elixir
Of the truth,
The hope and glory
Of your youth.
When your heart was beating
To the rhythm of life
And your life was dancing
To the beat of your heart.

Rod Trott

The Sibling

We'd play all day
My brother and I,
In summer till dusk
Then Mother would cry,

'Suppertime boys, it's getting late'
We'd finish the kick-about
And jump over the gate.

Inside the house
We'd wash and then eat,
My brother would
Always be first for the treat.

He'd race me to the table
And sit in my chair,
He'd pinch bits off my plate
Before I got there.

He was so funny
That brother of mine,
He played all sorts of tricks
All of the time.

Then one day
Right out of the blue,
His behaviour started changing,
I didn't know what to do.

Around and around
In circles he'd go,
Stop and stare,
Didn't even say hello.

My brother, my brother,
It was very sad.
Autism took away
The best friend I ever had.

Patty Rogers

Sound Senses - Sunset

Reflect through the storm,
The giant terrain
Galloping horses sound,
Hearts pound
Into the world of doom
It comes all too soon.
Reflection blooms,
When stars shine.
Through from the gate of Hell
The shell of true love -
Flies a beautiful white dove . . .
The universe of truth
Soothes
And reflection smiles . . .
Over the stile unseen
The mile amongst flowers
Little ladybird dreams
Escape from pain -
Time to sleep again
Away from the reflections
Past.
Through the mirror away
The greengage . . .
Little stream trickling
Poetry strives the living
Amongst the musical harps
Triumph the past.
The future will always live
And give
Happiness.

Josie Lawson

The River Of Time

The river of time rages, like a maelstrom through your head,
Your body reels from the hate of a million living dead,
And your mind is swirling swiftly, in tears of the truth,
As a thousand bitter memories haunt you from your youth.

Your future days have all been erased, weeks and long months too,
What happened to those great years that were spread in front of you?
For when you were a lonely child you schemed your life away,
The innocence of childhood had no place upon your day.

You battled through your teens and the world was your deadly foe,
Unseen enemies conspiring, to cut your green grass low.
A hundred nights of passion, the sound of a breaking heart,
Left you with an emptiness that would tear your life apart.

Was marriage of convenience, convenient enough?
With your soul and body shackled to a golden handcuff.
You took a thousand lovers and they took you for a ride,
And rampaging through your conscience they slew your
                                            precious pride.

Poverty rests easy on a head where a crown has slipped
For the absence of security meant your heels were clipped.
The distance from the sidewalk, to the gutter beneath your feet,
A measure of the circumstance, between winning and defeat.

Now you are the poorer, from the farewells of your rich friends,
Life is worth nothing without the substance that makes amends.
The lonely path you walk, takes you close to the river's edge.
There you stare with dead eyes, as you stand on the crumbling ledge.

Your body tells you to stop but your mind wants you to fly,
So you fall beneath the dark waves knowing here you will lie,
In this bubbling callous cauldron, called the river of time
And here you will listen to the funeral bell's last chime.

Raylton Dixon

Seven Deadly Sins

Some say there are seven deadly sins
They're all around us and they come from deep within.
How they come into this world I do not know
But many millions seem to follow.
Why is it that we experience these?
We run through them with heaps of ease,
Close your eyes and visualise a world without lies.
How can a person grow with these surroundings?
In a sea of sins we find ourselves drowning.
The world is very vague
And these sins are like the plague.
An infection or disease,
They spread like a million fleas.
What sick puppets we are
From virtuosity we have drifted so far.
Are since used as teaching tools?
How can God be so cruel?
A sin a day, seven a week, three hundred and sixty-five in a year,
So many sins make my vision blur.
It makes me think, is there such a thing as perfection?
Is it a sin to use protection?
Well, all I can say is
That sins aren't the way.
Life is choice,
God is the voice.
Prevention is the key
To stop animosity.
That's about all the advice I can give you
Believe and you'll see what He above can do.

Mavrinder Singh Dhothar

Everything For The Office

'Everything for the office'
That's what the catalogue said.
But to be absolutely precise
It now conjures up feelings of dread.

Now available in great quantity
So many products are on display.
All of the highest quality
I honestly must say.

'Twas then I noticed one product especially,
Thinking of myself, *I'll have one of those.*
I need to make this product mine officially,
It was expensive the one I chose.

And so the seeds of ownership were planted,
This old one needs some serious repair.
Then ordering the one I wanted,
My own brand new office chair.

July the 2nd, my swivel chair arrived,
Hurriedly, removing packaging and such.
Oh good, although dropped once or twice, it survived,
I love my brand new chair very much.

Gracefully sitting myself upon it,
I joyfully started to swivel round and round,
But now I'm feeling a right twit,
It kept on spinning until it became unwound.

Just as the boss walked in,
Suddenly I was flying through the air.
I was kicking up such an awful din,
Life really can be so unfair.

My legs wound around the boss' neck,
I was now his everlasting fan.
With the office staff all rushing around to check
And removing me from the boss as fast as they can.

They took my poor boss home,
As he wasn't feeling very well.
Complaining bitterly because he had come
In early, but suddenly developed a dizzy spell.

Next day he came back into work
Still looking so pale and wan.
He was feeling a proper berk
Disappearing into his office as fast as he can.

My boss then called me in
Gave me a right good telling off.
'Wipe off that silly grin
Fancy mobbing me in front of office staff.'

Then I started to get upset and cry,
For I was feeling small and ashamed.
Just then he gave out a sigh
And said then you really cannot be blamed.

He then took me home,
Comforted me and gave me a hug.
I really should not have gone,
Now I'm feeling a proper mug.

For now I am with child,
Of this there is no doubt.
I'm feeling so cross and wild
Because I'm looking kind of stout.

So when they say everything for the office,
My friends should be made aware.
I would recommend all of the office products
But not the bloody office swivel chair.

Josephine Smith

A Holiday In The Baltics

We went on a cruise to the Baltic Sea,
A fortnight's holiday, my husband and me.
Although I loved the countries and the weather was fine,
My husband was miserable, he did nothing but whine.

Everything was wrong, nothing was right,
Except for the oil rigs in the North Sea at night.
The people were stuffy, the music no good,
Dress up for dinner! I thought that he should.

Black and white night, he dressed in brown,
We went for a steak but his face had a frown.
Six chips on his plate this would not do,
He longed for a plateful, his intolerance grew.

The four-course dinner was delicious for me,
The waiter attentive, as efficient as could be.
For my husband, second sitting was rather too late,
Nothing ever tempted him, it was all second rate.

The classical concerts were all such a bore,
Dressing for dinner was another awful chore.
The elderly people got in his way,
He'd prefer it at home, at the end of the day!

The excursions were rushed, no time to look,
Getting onto coaches, what a long time it took.
He was happiest walking doing our own thing,
Lunch didn't matter; I took it on the chin.

Helsinki, my favourite, Oslo was great,
Discovering Copenhagen and Stockholm, couldn't wait.
Russia was interesting, Latvia old,
But these beautiful countries all left him cold.

A cruise to remember for me, not for him,
A shame that he found it so utterly grim!

June Melbourn

Beloved Peak District
(A poem about the Peak District, a place of great escape for those who live in the nearby industrial sprawls such as Stoke on Trent and Sheffield.)

From the estates and the junkies you are a way of escape
Fresh air in my nostrils, my deeper nature awakes.
I ascend up the bank past the roaches, the great gateway
To the great moorland landscape, an otherworldly infinity.

Sometimes when I get to the top, it is fog, mist and gloom
Nevertheless, I am filled with your tune
That tells me there is another worldly experience but a few miles away,
I wish I could live here, I wish I could stay.

I see the motorcyclists enjoying the thrill of the open road
Experiencing the great freedom for which the peak is known.
There are others who walk, some go to the pubs for real ale,
While I leave behind everything in the city that is stale.

In the winter there is snow, even when it is nowhere else.
Armed with the snowboard, taking advantage before it melts.
After we go to the Travellers Rest, steak and ale pie and chips,
Warming our fingers by the open fire before they fall to bits.

I go to Blackbrook Nature Reserve and I'm surrounded by deer,
But the last Friday of the month I go to the Winking Man pub for a beer.
The highest nightclub in the land, playing blistering rock
But the atmosphere is friendly, they don't run amok.

So next time you are sick of those grey streets of murk
Head for the Peak District when you're not at work.
Break away from the concrete sprawl and give it a chance
A place of great beauty, let us all make it last.

John Field

Search

Oh where can I find this love of mine?
My heart cries out through the sands of time.
Oh where can I see that sunlit smile?
Forever in my dreams it doth beguile.

Oh where can I hear that soft spoken word?
Which is more sweet than trilling bird.
Will I look each day in the morning dew
To see that love for strength anew?

Will I see that smile in summer's gentle rain
Or in a child's sweet face pressed to windowpane?
Will I hear that voice in the ocean's roar
As sea and surf caress distant shore?

My heart doth ponder this mystery,
Is the spirit winged with flight so free?
Will tomorrow I find the answer there?
Will it be answered by deed or by a prayer?

Oh where can I find this love so dear?
Which in my heart I hold so near.
Will memory hold fast, will reunion prove strong?
In that special place where we all belong.

Henrietta Valmore

3.33am

It's 3.33am in the morning and my mind is in a whirl,
been the same since childhood, since I was a very young girl.

I've tried counting sheep till I'm blue in the face,
had hot milk and biscuits - my weight's a disgrace.

Recently I've even succumbed to the vine,
and opened a bottle of full-bodied red wine.

Can anyone please give me a good reason,
why the time's the same whatever the season?

Is there something magic about that morning hour?
If so I'd really like to harness some elusive power.

I'd like to sleep right through the night,
awaking in the morning with head so clear and bright.

I'd polish off my chores so fast you'd not see me for dust,
instead I'm weary, listless, feel my body's made of rust.

It's just a plea for help in my nocturnal plight
cos sleeping through would make me a so much better sight!

Christine Bridson-Jones

Dreams Of Childhood

The day is nearly over
The night is drawing in
And shadows of the past
Will soon start to begin

The darkness starts to quicken
And the moon begins to glow
My head will hit the pillow
And dreams will start to flow

Of when I was a child
Warm and safe in bed
With my family close by
My toys spread around my head

My heart and mind delights
In the vision of the night
When the mystic magic realm
Links my sleep to sound and sight

From morning all through the day
In the garden with friends I play
Childhood, the kingdom of joy
Past memories caught in time

The doors reopen from the past
And my dreams come flowing in
So from night to early morn
My childhood dreams are reborn.

James Tracey-Burner

The Toxic Garden

In the toxic garden nothing dies
And immortality blooms;
The grass is pink, the trees are blue
Whether oak or birch or yew
Growing in copses and in combes
That enclose the toxic garden.

Hummingbirds the size of bats
Fly in the toxic garden,
And feast on yeasty nectar vats
In purple flowers the size of cats
And marvellous are these birds to see
Examples of ornithology
That live in the toxic garden.

Vast aphids live on lively plants
Where ants their interest advance
Imbibing aphid honey, a tasty item,
Which ants can drink ad infinitum.
In the toxic garden.

Poison lies in being chained
Forever in paradise,
Whilst beauty permanently ingrained
Becomes aesthetically stained
But by paradise may be regained
In the toxic garden.

Walter Harris

My Love

When you hold me close, so close to you,
It makes me feel so good inside,
You've made me feel a love that's new,
It feels stronger than an ocean tide.
When our lips meet and caress so smooth
You make me feel good in every way,
Your arms round me a perfect groove,
'I love you my darling' is what I say.
You're a perfect gentleman so hard to find
With a heart as big as the highest score,
You're beautiful, loving, so good and kind,
Everything about you I adore.
You're generous, thoughtful with a gentle touch,
You're gorgeous face, your loving eyes,
I love you my darling so very much
What I have just written isn't lies.

Leah Vernon

A Knight To Reply

'Oh Anne dear sweet
you know not I -
allow me to enlighten thy.

Your latest poem did my sire smite
he rages and froths at fortunes blight,
but how I notice your sweet scent
it can't be due to accident
that fate has brought us into touch,
your acquaintance I should very much
like to get to know.
I'm told by friend Ivanheave Hoe
that I'm a stoutly so and so -
and so I'll introduce thyself.
Sir Gladhehad, bids you good health.'

Andy Cameron

Young Forever

I wish I could be
Young forever
Or maybe just
All my life

Then I'd have
The lust for
Living
Until I found
A wife

We'd work hard every day
To carve the bread
With knife
And perhaps have
Lots of children
Who'd make us very happy
For all of our life
(But they do cost a lot!)

Christian Schou

The # Key

The # key on my keyboard
Annoys me every day,
It serves no use nor purpose
And just gets in my way.
Not once have I used it,
Not once in all my life.
I only press it by mistake,
Which causes stress and strife.
Seeing how it's meaningless
An utter waste of space,
Surely now, the time has come,
To remove that # disgrace.

Matthew R Worthington

Who Does The Cooking In Your House?

What do you do with yourself all day?
Sardonic smile in empathy.
Don't you get bored?
Superior smile in sympathy.
You do the school run . . . and then what?
There's nothing much else to do after that.
 . . . Why, I stay at home in apathy . . .
Why?
Why does it bother you?
Sarcastic grin in sympathy.

My partner goes off to work at seven-thirty precisely -
To earn the bread, bring home the bacon, put food on the table
                                                  for the family;
I do the school run then come home to sit . . . in atrophy,
To bask in apposite atrophy.
I do the school run then come home to play,
To fritter away . . . to idle away the empty hours
On the garden, the cleaning, the cooking, the shopping,
                                            the household chores . . .
 . . . On a litany of little tasks too general to enumerate,
Too boring for you to contemplate.
(Save that every action is equal and opposite.)

Me, I'd get bored sitting around the house all day:
(With nothing to do except to play at being mother).
Then, when my daughter innocently calls me Mummy,
Those besuited fathers, duty done at the school gate, hurry
Their weight from one foot to the other,
Exchange knowing nods with their besuited brothers
With eyebrow raised in disapproval, scoff,
Unsettled by the gender issue, and scurry off
To the office to play . . . at work:
(To play at work . . . I know, I've been there . . . I used to play
                                              in the real world, dork).

I do the school run then come home to six empty hours
Of sitting on my arse with a gin and tonic in a soundless house.
I do the school run then come home to twiddle my thumbs,
                                        to contemplate my belly,
Mentally, physically, emotionally, in front of the telly
In boredom,
In freedom.
I do the school run then come home to six hours of lethargy.
I don't live in the real world!
Me, I never get bored lounging in my irresponsibility,
Superior smile in sympathy.

Ian Lowery

Why Me?

Why is it I
who holds all in my hands?
Why is it I?
I was not born to be lord of these lands.
Why me?
Was this how my life was meant to be?
Why have I no true destiny?
I held firm for years,
suffered all with grace, no tears.
Why me?
Like a weary warrior, I want to lay down my sword,
I want to experience, find the real me,
surely this isn't how life's supposed to be.
I've fought unwinnable battles,
I've stood firm and tall,
but now I have to say I have had enough of it all.
My life's been one long struggle,
I want now to enjoy all,
it's not a lot to ask, infact, it's rather small.
I've not given up, just reality has set in,
I can never change anything, as life is just grim.
No words I say, sinks in other's ears,
even the ones I have held closest and so dear.
Why me?

Karen Dennis

Ps & Queues

The other day while in a store
I saw a sign that said 'Ay here'
And so with little else to do I joined the aying queue,
The queue that would enable me to ay.

Together with the other ayers
The players, soothsayers, vampire slayers
I shuffled forward in the queue
Until it was my turn to ay.

But the sales assistant looked at me
Uncomfortably when I went 'Ay'
'Eh?' he say,
'Ay,' I say.
Then 'Ayyyy! Ayyyy! Ayyyy!
Look at me, I can go ay. I can, I can.
It says, 'Ay here' and so I ay, yay, yeah.'

'No way!'
'No way, no way, no way,' he say
'That's not the way to ay,
You need a cheque or cash or card,
Or if you like I can fetch the guard.'
'But it says . . .'
'That's not what's meant!'

Despondently, I turned away,
Only then to hear him say,
'Not so flipping clever now, eh?
Not so ruddy big.
Silly -illock, false -retender
-est and -ompus -rig.'

Christopher Melhuish

Geordieland

Geordies are friendly folk,
They live around the River Tyne,
Newcastle is their city,
I'm proud to say it's mine.
No matter where you come from,
You're always welcome here,
Before you've introduced yourself,
They've taken you for a beer.
A smile lights up their faces
When they talk about their roots,
How they walked the Jarrow March for work,
Mud caked on clothes and boots.
The finest ships were built here,
Coal hewn from deep-filled mines,
Their eyes mist over as they tell you
Not hard to read between the lines.
Then someone mentions football,
Newcastle's pride and joy,
Jackie Milburn, Alan Shearer,
Avid fans since they were boys.
Famous landmarks can be seen here,
Tyne Bridge; The Sage; to name but a few,
The Magpies, brown ale and stotty cake,
Are Geordie through and through.
But what makes Tyneside people special
Is the warm welcome they extend,
Whenever strangers arrive here
They always leave as friends.

Marion Brown

My Brave Little Man

How do we abort pain?
To separate it from a puzzled brain.
Through anger and frustration, nothing can I gain,
You'll understand if your child's in pain.

When I saw his swollen and bloodied face,
I wished I was in his place.
My heart doing somersaults began to race,
How did this happen in the first place?

'I'm alright Mum,' spoke my little man.
He had fallen off his dad's van.
Emotions around my mind ran,
Why has this happened to my little man?

Time's a great healer so they say
But it didn't help take the pain away.
Into the hospital to see him each day
He understood I couldn't stay.

Four days later he came home,
I couldn't bear to leave him alone.
All through his pain he didn't groan,
For me many a time did I moan.

The worst of it we have overcome,
Nearly all the hospital checks we have done.
I have been so proud of my son,
I don't know from where his strength has come.

A family closer we have become,
Many things will be left undone.
To replace the hurt we need fun,
This is a challenge we have won.

About it all I am still miffed
In time our pain and anger will lift,
All this from our memories will drift
Life is the *most precious gift*.

Carol Paxton

Life Is A Blackberry

Life is a blackberry waiting for you
unknown as black, bright as sundew.
Small as a bullet, hard with it too,
mangled, fly-eaten, bitter right through.
Or full to the bursting, it bleeds at your touch
giving its all too soon and too much.

Life is a bramble, that is for sure,
a challenge to find us out evermore.
It tempts us to folly, stings us to pain,
then invites us to do it all over again.
It stays out of reach, so clearly in view,
it dazzles our eyes and we plummet anew.
When we fall to the thorns, a black berry we meet
it was sitting right there, all the time, at our feet.

Juicy with dew from summer's long quest,
its low place means nothing. It's one of the best.
Yet the high one we find is not nearly so fine
as when we first glimpsed it above in the sun.

Delusion dressed up in a fruity disguise,
an autumnal joke full of surprise.
Not just for the jams, jellies and pies
but to help us live life and smile at its lies.
Ready to show us the way back to Earth,
to alter our thinking, question the worth
of all that we see and all that we hear
in gathering in the fruits of the year.

Ann Palmer

She

She looks at you and hopes for something more,
But she's another one of them that you ignore.
That girl, you think, is nothing like the rest,
In fact, I'd say she's only second best.
She listens and writes down everything you say
In the hope that you'll be hers someday.
Then you turned around, said, 'I don't love her.'
She would like you to give something to her.
She says too much and sometimes hates herself,
Begins the long journey up to your shelf.
Then you push her off and she starts to fall,
You walk away cos you don't care at all.
She wishes she could say it to your face,
There's just not the right time or the right place.
The girl is running before she has to leave,
Maybe she doesn't know what to believe.
She wants to turn back the clock to the past,
Start again; make it all not go so fast.
There would be no need to feel what she felt,
She could cope so much better with what she was dealt.
She passes you by in the corridor,
You give her nothing worth fighting for.
But she doesn't want to lose what she's found
That's why she's still her, standing her ground.
All she wants is for you to hear her out
Even though you don't know what it's about.
She doesn't want to tell you once again,
You think it's all about her and her pain.
Those three words she says mean nothing
Yet, she wants them to mean anything.
She somehow has to say to you goodbye
And pray that she doesn't start to cry.
She doesn't want to but she doesn't have a choice,
Can you hear her screaming, her yelling voice?
She's only got a few days left to live
And she doesn't have that much more to give.
She's looking at you and hoping for something more,
Maybe this time she'll be the one you won't ignore.

Beth Harmston

The Dream Tunnel

I am walking in the wilderness,
The wilderness of my life.
Entering through the darkest tunnels
Why am I in such strife?

Through every frightening twist and turn,
With huge cobwebs surrounding me,
Gripping me until I tripped and fell
Then struggled to break free.

In a panic now I shout for help,
But there is no one there to hear.
My heart is pounding, my pulse is fast,
Is there anyone to really care?

Then at the darkest point in time,
I saw a ray of golden light,
As I approached from whence it came,
I knew this way to go was right.

For within that golden ray of light,
I saw a vision that was you,
Waiting there to comfort me,
Just as you used to do.

As I drew nearer into your outstretched arms
I saw the smile upon your face.
I felt your kiss, your gentle touch,
And your comforting warm embrace.

Gradually then your vision faded,
Tears like a river were running down my face.
For a little while we had been together,
The tunnel then became a happier place.

As I awoke, once more alone,
Emerging from the tunnel of my dream,
I know now you are watching over me
Until the day we meet again.

Maud Eleanor Hobbs

September Rain

Watching the day disappear,
The restless rain does fall
Upon the ground.
Reflecting the night in the city,
In the vast, tall place
That I am found.

Silence fills the empty streets.
I've passed this way before,
Time and again.
Walking to a place called nowhere
In the cold, dark dank
September rain.

I watch the advertising signs
Changing to the heartbeat
Of the night.
Colours of the brands and logos
On the large wide boards
Do shine so bright.

They try to hypnotise my mind
But they have no meaning,
They're just a stain
On the city that now is sleeping
Through the cold, dark, dank
September rain.

Andrew Blakemore

Timing

An hour of confusion.
Half-asleep,
to me it felt like illusion.
It's that time of year
when the clocks are changed.
Which way, is far from clear!
Like the seasons
and so many reasons,
yes, a time of confusion.
Spring growth all around
brilliant sunshine and birdsong abound.
Yet, this is autumn,
wrapped in greenery and perfumed roses,
my garden in wondrous confusion,
bathed in an azure-blue sky,
clear and high.
Early morning tea, outside,
enjoying the natural world in spring like voice,
in-between 'hours'
till the distant indoor radio
announced the 8am news!
Ah yes, I should remember,
backwards for autumn.

Margaret Ann Wheatley

The Calm'r Mind

Wint'r breeze
Through barren trees,
The time of year
When all does freeze;
The cloudless sky
So stark, so bold,
As the page on which
Disquiet thoughts unfold;
And of such thoughts
The moods that come,
Admit no discourse
With the hours of sun;
The sable hours
The dreams of yore,
Mine power beholds
All things and more;
The calm'r mind
Focus'd within,
Perceives beyond the silence
To the souls that sing;
Such introspection
Is most correctly short,
For more lengthy tours
Subtle dangers court;
For the barren mind
Fears not the breeze,
That strips dark thoughts
As wint'r leaves;
Yet fears itself
When the mood is done,
When reality reigns
When e'en demons run.

M Sam Dixon

Daisies And Buttercups

'Daisies are our silver,
Buttercups our gold.'
This is what in Sunday School,
We tiny tots were told.

But now, prized with the ideal lawn,
Sown with expensive seeds,
Buttercups (and daisies too),
I've come to loathe as weeds.

But maybe Sunday School was right,
As Wordsworth knew - in sum:
'Trailing clouds of glory (half-
Remembered) do we come.'

May daisies be our silver
And buttercups our gold.
For these words are the wisest
Ever known or told.

Alan Millard

Always, Always Do

I tried to keep it a secret
But I couldn't keep it from you
You knew just how to reach it
You always, always do

You disarmed me with your charm
I wanted to hug you
You sheltered me from harm
You always, always do

The atmosphere was electric
A current around you
You love and protect me
You always, always do

Daniel White

Count Your Blessings

Happiness around you.

A pot of tea for you and me or coffee if you prefer
It would be nice to sit in peace if that is too on offer
No dog to bark at those who walk past
Or cat to chase . . . is that too much to ask?
Maybe they're blessings too in disguise
Which we should come to realise
And give thanks for the fun and love they bring
As another day dawns and we hear birds sing.
In a favourite place like a woodland stream
Where to walk is a delight - and for sure some dream
Is made amidst the sweet sounds all around
Whilst busy little creatures scurry underground.

So many times joys unaware abound
To amaze and astound - great minds they confound.
The work of our Creator of Man here below
No matter what trials he may undergo . . .
So many blessings - beautiful and free
Countless and wonderful . . . like the silver sea
In the moonlight under a starlight sky
Which no man could make . . . neither you nor I.
Nor the brilliant sunset whether pink, red or gold
Priceless blessings, abundant - so many to behold.

A blessing may come as another one goes
Whilst flower growing freely as does the wild rose.
Adding to all colours of autumn, winter and spring
To continue into summer - of nature's own making
With the hedgerows ablaze in colour of every hue,
Blessings a-plenty for me and for you.
But do we realise how poorer we'd be
Without so much colour and beauty to see?
Or those newborn lambs which seem to say
Be glad . . . be happy, I've arrived today!

So as snowdrops grow anew and bluebells too
Or as new baby's breath breathes on you
And whilst the bride and groom still says, 'I do'
May love precious and true - forever stay
Through all tears and laugher we meet on our way.

Irene A Dalzell

Reflection

Every direction I turn, I see the image I despise
Clutching at my heartstrings, no one hears my cries
Staring back at me all I see is hatred
Something once perfect, is now so cold and tainted

Make-up covered the evil that lurked beneath her skin
And thoughts of anger and malice behind that innocent grin
The act she has perfected, throughout all the years
Is seeping through slowly confirming all her fears

She's crippled from the pain inflicted upon her soul
As it bubbles up inside her she struggles to keep control
All she feels is envy for the person she once obtained
She's helpless in this world, she feels emotionally drained

She tries to rid the guilt of what she has become
And every inch of her just wants to scream and run
There is no path to change this beaten heartless complexion
The image staring back is my mirrored reflection.

Daisy Wells

Sadness

He has sad lonely eyes
Which no one can see,
His laughter fools everyone
Everyone but me.

His mind is troubled
His world upside down,
On the outside a smile
But inside a frown.

His body lives on
His mind is dead,
While we see sunlight
He sees red.

His childhood is over
But life is not,
He's now just empty
An empty pot.

He could have had help
If he'd been able to see,
One person caring
That person was me.

Natalie Mallory

Live And Let Live

Live and let live
The way our world should be
Freedom for you
Freedom for me
Freedom for all
Be you black
Be you white
Freedom for all
It's only right.

Alan Green

Round 100

Why am I in this fight again
I ask myself
resting between boxing
bouts with you.

I have to keep my gloves up high
the body blows
come thick and fast and you
fight dirty.

I'm black and blue, I ache
but still
we keep the punches coming
glove after bloody glove
they call it love.

Helen Crick

Hobbies

Some people do embroidery,
Some crochet with a hook,
Some do fancy knitting
With a pattern from a book.

Others make nice pictures
With shells gathered from the shore,
Clever folks write stories
Or sculpt or paint or draw.

I'm in a different category
For when I have the time,
I like to jot my thoughts down
And try to make them rhyme.

Lily Wilding

Say Goodbye

A murmur whispers through the trees
As day turns into night
Shadows dance on the fallen leaves
As I watched her walk out of sight.

Our problems seem to overwhelm us
The grief goes too deep
Tears lay dry upon our cheeks
The future will have to keep.

The loss of our child brings us such pain
How can we go on?
As she walks towards his final resting place
The wind seems to sing a song.

God is still with you my friends
Even if you are sad
Your child has been taken home again
But you will always be his dad.

So remember the good times you had
The smiles and chuckles he gave
Love was given for such short a time
The sacrifice has to be made.

God has called your child back home
To His loving arms once more
Your love made him but God wanted him too
He knows your heart is sore.

You will meet one day soon you know
In another time and place
But your love will continue to grow
In dreams you will see his face.

Sue Godsell

My Wonderful Mum

Who would have thought I could have a mum like you
I don't even know but I know it's true

You are my world, my angel in fancy dress,
I love you so much so here's what I'll confess.

You're the best in so many ways,
You'd walk me to school and watched my plays.

You would tuck me in bed and I was gently kissed
I'd fall fast asleep, my mum I missed.

I went to college after school,
Some of the students were so cruel.

You would go in and have a word,
Not another sound was ever heard.

I passed my course, you were so pleased,
I knew now I was clever, I wouldn't be teased.

You've been there, through thick and thin
Put me first, it was never, 'In a min!'

Now I'm older, happy and wise,
I've done this poem as a big surprise.

Money, presents, cards are alight,
But nothing compares to my delight.

I love you in so many ways
And always will for the rest of my days.

I love you Mum, Steph.

Stephanie Leese

Street Singer

Deserted early morning promenade
Save for a street sweeper from LA
Uninhibited and unpretentiously
Singing unaccompanied, 'My Way'

Amply assisted by the force of gravity
An improved device of brush and bin
He was absorbed in giving his performance
Unaware that I was listening in.

No attempt to imitate the great Sinatra
Or be recognized for his vocal gift
Still less to be made the butt of humour
Or be mocked, or be given the short shift

Just a statement of comfort and contentment
The hero and leading role in his time
Pouring out his soul in a personal best -
A triumph in performing the sublime.

Should I continue on my intended path
Intruding with my presence on his day
To clumsily bring him down to earth
Or tenderly sneak out of his way.

Kevin Power

Waves Wash Over Me

Waves wash over me as I lie on the shore,
Chilling my mind and cleansing my core.
Refreshing my thoughts of how things turn around,
As I sit here on the sandy wet ground.

Sitting in wonder as the time slips away
Just how tiny I am in this vast open bay.
How lost and alone, how tranquil, serene,
How peaceful it is from what my life has been.

The sunlight is fading, day turns to night,
As I sit in the darkness under a pale moonlight.
Watching the glisten and twinkling glow
Of stars and the planets, the beauty on show.

Minutes turn to hours as I am lost in a gaze,
Caught up in the darkness, immersed in the haze.
My thoughts drifting along as if moved by the tide
Washing away memories I have tried to hide.

The cooling night air, a breeze so sublime,
Lost in a moment, captured in time.
Waves wash over me as I lie on the shore
Chilling my mind and refreshing my core.

Neil Renwick

Back To The Sea

Back to the sea
You and me
We live between each wave
Fish look us in the eye
And tell us what we left behind.

It's a cruel mountain
Full of tales and celebration
We all like fish and chips
Crabs and prawns under the moon.

When we are asleep
People are working,
Living on a boat
Dreaming of God knows what.
This sea can be cruel
And warm, full of love and pleasure

Will the sea ever end?
Who shall sail in its last boat?
Who shall cast the last net?
Remember, two days off
Then back to sea
You and me.

Who shall sleep
First or last?
This sea is in your mind and heart
Remember that and hold your head high.

Kenneth Mood

Wildlife

Thank you David Attenborough
For all your wildlife features,
You've opened so many eyes
To such amazing creatures.
Your deep seabed photography
Has really reached its peak,
One stops to wonder, constantly,
Are there more sights to seek?
Blue Planet, left us all spellbound
As you searched the oceans deep,
Of all the strange sea creatures found
That swim or crawl or creep.
New birds or fish or animals,
I suppose there's more to find,
But surely Mr Attenborough,
Has found mostly every kind.
It's possible, however,
He may find something new,
An undiscovered creature
That hopped or swam or flew.
And so we watch his programmes
In hopes, that just in case,
David finds a species new
Until then, watch this space!

Derek Tanton

Talent

I can't paint you a pretty scene,
a raging sea or island dream.
I can't paint visions that I see,
I've no talent, you must agree.

Nonsense, this is all in your mind
yours a talent of practical kind.
You make your garden come to bloom
knowing when to plant or prune.

If you're no creator of art
but can replace a car's part,
or dress some can easily make
or feather light sponge others bake.

We each have a talent to use
so no one has a good excuse.
Just ask yourself where lies my talent
then have fun and experiment.

Valerie Ovais

Wonderment

I know I am lucky to live where I do
Surrounded by sea and countryside too.
Often I go for long walks on the beach
And the names of shells my granddaughter teach.

Or walk along flower-decked country lanes
Several species of flora explain.
Love look of wonderment on young one's face
Footprints of animals fervently trace.

Delight exploring rock pools, that's a must,
Young one would stay enthralled from dawn to dusk.
In her excitement I've always covered,
Thankful this peaceful abode I discovered.

Susan Mullinger

Tribute To North East Coal Miners

Black as night where all sounds are muffled
Down on knees crawling men have shuffled,
Working and labouring to bring folk coal
Deep underground working in endless hole

What this reflects are men hard and refined
Able to cope as the images here have defined,
Coping was severe when the work was all gone
Coal mines, coal miners, these days are near none

Sportsmen and footballers are paid a mere fortune
Yet those risking lives are all forgotten too soon,
Skimping, scraping just trying to make ends meet
They were the heroes we should bow at their feet.

Without them the day, where would all Geordies be
Only those understanding can read this and yet see
The pain and the suffering endeared by those men
Will live on in endless hearts until time says when.

C Slater

Tears

My tears that fall
Are tears of joy
For our little boy
Who has just been born
Into this world
He will grow
And learn a world of knowledge
Of tears, joy, peace and harmony
So when he grows
He will have manners
So keep him safe, keep him close
And you will gain the most.

Deborah Storey

Cancer Ward

He lay in a drugged sleep in the cancer ward
With drug induced dreams he didn't get bored
The family came to see him every visiting time
And sat with him in silence until the bell's chime
His wife was in torment and his children so sad
For the man that they loved, her husband, their dad

They didn't want to leave
They didn't want to grieve

For he was dying a lonely man's death
As he alone fought for every last breath
He couldn't bear to open his eyes and look at their faces so taut in pain
Yet knowing they were there, he felt that his life hadn't been in vain
To see him suffering so much was painful to watch
The nurse shook her head and looked at her fobwatch

His wife had given him children of which he was very proud
He said, 'Thank you' these were the last words he said aloud
He didn't want to leave all those to whom he'd given his love
But God decided to bring him home on the wings of a dove
As his soul soared high above the bed and the sheet
It all seemed to him to be so bittersweet.

To be free at last of all his pain and medication
But sorry to leave those behind who'd given him such dedication
Yet he was going to a better place as he knew he must
And allow his loved ones to recover was fair and just
He whispered a prayer as he looked down on them
'Now all of you that I love can rest in peace - Amen.'

Elizabeth Ann Farrelly

Retirement January 31st 2007

Do we dream of retirement and how we will spend our time?
Oh yes, oh yes, oh yes we do!
Each day arising, we've duties to fulfil
Maybe our choices are not all we desire.
But again our daily tasks are all we may have to do
Giving people their choices and desires in life
To make them happy too.
We may be sure that we are all needed through and through
Time flies by so quickly, the years get shorter too
And then we begin to wonder
What our retirement time will tempt each to do?
Time we spend with people from other lands and seas
The nature of our plants hold so many secrets too.
Secrets to behold and marvel at so
The lambs, the sea, the sky
Why should they pass us by?
People meeting people of every walk of life
Have so much to share about their lives
And so we become wiser and wiser
To share with them our thoughts
Although life and time slips quickly by
We reach our destination where we have to say goodbye
Memories we leave with them
Some happy and some sad
But these we love they will treasure
Whether they are happy or sadly, sadly sad.

Thelma Jean Crossham Everett

Together Again

She's been wanting love forever
Yeah sure seems a long, long time
From one day to one week
Then from year until next year
Love seems to be round everywhere else
Everywhere else but here

He says not to fall in love
She's not the type to give a man her heart
So he hopes that she might change
That he might go and be the one
Everyone else says they're in love
And he might be the one she wants

Be true to her for she needs love
And she wants him to be her man
Love should never be complicated
It should be something we can understand

He thinks she's so childish
She's more grown up than she acts
A burning ear tells me
That she's talking about me now
Whispering love to her closest friend
We'll be together somehow.

Rodger Moir

Norman

Where Norman goes
No one knows,
To last the day is his main aim
He starts out drunk and stays the same.

The hours fade in and out of his mind
We might as well be dumb or blind
To passers-by who look through him
He sees through them with eyes turned dim.

Survival deals him dirty days
Survival seen through an alcohol haze.
A scavenger for litter bins
Makes his mark midst lager tins.

Burrowing beneath the waste and dirt
Finds his meal, the triumph hurts.
Bacon rind and apple peel
For once tonight he's made his deal.

As meantime melts into lean time
The wind blows up his nose
Where Norman goes
No one knows.

Gary Austin

An Inconvenient Spoof

I've paved my front garden and planted three cars,
The rain cannot reach underground reservoirs.

But I just don't believe what they say are our follies
That the poles are now melting like two big ice lollies.

Great Yarmouth, it sizzles like somewhere in France
And scorpions are spreading all over Northants.

The warmest year yet since records began. It
Was the hottest one yet on our little planet.

The forests are falling in the Amazon Basin,
But I just won't acknowledge the problems we're facing.

So I've bought me a Hummer and I drive it around,
I know that it's not ecologically sound.

I hog all the roads form St Albans to Peckham,
And I boast that I've got one just like David Beckham.

I'll read a newspaper that questions the proof
That this warming is global and not just a spoof.

I'll battle my corner and hold my position
I don't give a toss about carbon emissions.

Why should I be bothered or remotely concerned?
I'm just reaping the benefits of what I have earned.

Recycling is barmy; the greens are just daft,
Composting is something at which to be laughed.

Wind turbines are hideous; they're not the solution,
I prefer nuclear waste and industrial pollution.

No time for soul-searching, no time to reflect.
It's just all those pinkos being politically correct.

So please just ignore me when the sea starts to rise,
Don't throw me a line when it's up to my eyes.

Inconvenient truth or elaborate farce?
Now excuse me while I disappear . . .

Rob Barratt

Learning And Trust

I have learned that no matter what is promised
some people will always do what they believe,
I have learned that no matter how much I tell them that's wrong
these people will leave you to grieve.

I have learned that no matter how much I trust
that trust must be earned,
I have learned that when I tell them my trust is not on demand
why is it me who always gets his fingers burned?

I have learned never to compare myself to others
they are more confused than they will ever say,
I have learned that when I tell them that is not me
they will always tell me theirs is the better way.

I have learned that when they say, 'Trust me'
they mean until they are out of sight,
I have learned that most of these people are confidence tricksters
and for politicians that should not be right.

I have learned that we are responsible for what we do
unless we are politicians who profess to do no wrong,
I have learned that these men are not there to keep their promises
only to make us the public dance to their song.

Jim Anderton

Everywhere

I was walking on the dark side of the moon
When I saw a star go out
And it made one think of you.
Your strength, you give me each and every day
And, I'm in debt to you, don't you think . . .
I'll say goodnight but hopefully you'll give me another day
So I can play on this living, magical, spinning planet
You gave to us to share.

Pedi Fribence

Looking In From Without

As I lay with my head bathed in white
There lies next to me a man of whom I know not
We share laughter, hollow days, pitiless nights
We face identical climbs, ever climbing the face.

We've dreamed the same dreams, divided the fears
Slipstreaming life. Slowly picking the lock
Memories swing loose, betraying the years
Racing to win, never winning the race.

In silent chaos I drown. He's drowning too
Lost, we are both, in a plan long forgot
Which of us senses the path to pursue?
Does a dream life exist - or is life made of dreams?

One and the same or spirits apart?
Break free from myself? I know I cannot
Unravel my head or ripen my heart?
It seems I'm a stranger - as strange as it seems.

A whispering shout
Looking in from without.

Chris Sullivan

You And I

As I watched you lie there
With the morning sun shimmering on your face,
With your soft golden locks of hair,
Your chest rising and falling with such grace.
I wanted to reach over and hold you ever so tight,
But waking you would be like committing a crime.
Your face is that of an angel's in the morning light,
I wish this moment would last forever frozen in time.
My mind is drunk on your beautiful soul,
We belong together you and I,
Apart we are nothing but together we are whole,
I stroke your cheek and let out a harmonious sigh.

Kimberly Harries

Questions And Answer

Hold back the spoon I'll feed no more
Your beginning has no end
Your room has no door
You say no one can lose
I see that no one can win
The game of life holds back the tears
With an incongruous grin
Withering goals to proceed three steps
One to learn, one to try
And the third is regrets
To be asked what I know would count
But alas they ask me I don't
Somewhere a farmer harvests a thought
Somewhere a soldier weeps for the way he fought
Both their lives ruled by love and hate
Both their lives put down by fate.

James Thomas Rodbourn

Hyper Happy

I'm really hyper happy today
Even though everything hasn't gone my way
I just want to smile and sing
In my ears the music does ring
So I dance around my living room
And over cute boys I do swoon
Even though I am nearly twenty-one
I just want to have some giggling fun
And add in an adult glass of wine
While I sit and paint these nails of mine
I'm going to do my hair
And dress up without a care
Because I'm really hyper happy today
And I really love feeling this way.

Kim Davies

Jamie Through The Looking Glass

If ever a minute comes to pass
When I'm bored, uninspired
Or feel I won't last
Only one thing to do
Absolutely
It's true
Is to listen to a blast of
Philip Glass

With a flurry of notes
It becomes quite hypnotic
An aural variation
Of the burlesque and erotic

A rhythm or counterpoint
Jaunty and spiked
Jagged and punchy
Unusual, inventive
Eccentric, surreal
- But what's the big deal?
Some cry from top
To which I regale
- You ignorant fopp! -

This is the master of music
King of the chords
A hero of harmony
- Orchestra rattles the stage
And shudders the boards! -
It's vital with vitality
So many shades and tones
Gleaning new subtleties
On your fiftieth listen
(Like tasty new meat off
Thought-of-dead bones)

It's funky and fresh
Yet classically cool
Distorted yet recognisable
Like looking through a prism
- This is, after all
The Messiah of Minimalism!

His energy's contagious
The style I adore
In his company your life
Is never a bore
To listen, absorb
Swamped within sounds
Is never a chore
(I don't know how I survived
Without him before)
Each soundbite motif
Every musical cell
Has a pungent and urgent
Story to tell

Tender and loving
Stormy and fierce
Mysterious and dramatic
With four notes he'll pierce
Into your very soul essence
That primitive core
That makes you question
All that's gone before

Tickling with fingers
On the back of your neck
A musical seduction
A chromatic vignette
With a flute or a trumpet
A cello or harp
It's magical what he can conjure
With a simple G-sharp

With imagination and style
One can easily see
- If not understand how he does it -
This grand musico-illusionist's
Fantastical alchemy.

Jamie Caddick

Smile

We are losing the art of smiling;
the human race that is.
Unique to just our species,
it's a sin we cannot forgive.
Facial expressions are a gift to us;
a fact, that all must know.
So why is it I wonder,
smiling comes oft too slow?
Just like 'please' and 'thank you',
a smile costs nought at all.
And for sure a blank expression,
is like a bare brick wall!
Will smiling 'crack' your countenance;
somehow, do you harm?
Don't be naïve or foolish,
as indeed it will enhance your charm.
Worry, shows as crease and wrinkle,
ages all, before our time.
So forget all cares and worries,
let your smile - on others, shine!

Peter Mahoney

Waiting

What are we waiting for?
God only knows,
The bus or the train,
Or anything that goes.

We may be waiting for someone
Whom we have never seen
Or maybe it's different
Life, is just one dream.

But anyway, we wait and wait,
And then, it comes along.
Maybe we don't really know
For it could be a song.

E Holcombe

If I Had A Coin (Or Two)

My husband got us in a lot of debt
Nothing spent on me,
My daughter's getting ill
I don't get paid you see.

Our neighbours want our trees cut down
They're fifty foot high,
Trust us to get a house
With trees in the sky.

Money, money, money,
I got a second job, trying to clear the mess
The car is now in trouble
I'm trying my best.

They changed my hours in my job
No buses run that early,
Now I need the car
I can't afford to fix.

I'm wondering what to do now as they say
The car may or may not pull through,
It's fifty-fifty, toss a coin
If I had a coin or two.

Tracey McDicken

Sir John

Come back Sir John from yonder towers
and view the situation,
use all your supernatural powers
and enlighten this congregation.
Had you the dump never espied
come friendly bombs you'd not have cried
and to all those who had yet to come
would have remained silent
and wisely dumb.

David Thomas

If

If my eyes do open
When this dawn breaks through
Things I have to give
For things I want to live
To get me on these tracks
This roller coaster I will climb
These dreams they can be mine

I will sit up in these dodgems
And get knocked in life
Then I will climb out
This jackpot I can see
The fruit machines keeps rolling
To try to get my dreams

Ghost trains I can enter
My hair will stand on end
This entrance is in sight
For me to live my life.

The big wheel I will sit in
It will go round and round
Circles in my mind
For things I have to find
To climb out of this seat
More circles I can find
My life I try my best
For things I have to do
The merry-go-round keeps turning
There are things for me and you.

M B Tucker

Things In Life

Daisy chain
Rolling train
Bench and chairs
Grizzly bears
Lots of money
Sweet taste of honey
Socks and shoes
Games - you lose!
Fire log
Cat and dog
Dressing gown
Stairs going down
Our own warm home
A brush and comb
And don't forget
A garden gnome
A bird house
A squeaking mouse
A post and lamp
Dry and damp
Red, red wine
A dinosaur spine
Drunken men
A one-legged hen
A nice soft bed
A loaf of bred
The alphabet
From A to Z.

Olivia Griffiths

The Answer To Everything

A wise old sage and mystic
Looked deeply into me
'What's the answer to everything?'
He asked most solemnly.

I contemplated, meditated
And thought quite seriously,
And then I said, 'I know this one!
It's a nice cup of tea.'

He looked quite shocked
His world was rocked,
'It's true,' I said with glee.
The answer to everything
Is a nice cup of tea.

A death in the family?
Put the kettle on.
The celebration of a birth?
Lapsang Souchong.

Been taken to the cleaners
By your financial guru?
Lost everything you own?
 . . . One lump or two?

She's been jilted at the alter
On this, her wedding day.
Oh my goodness, poor old thing
Cup of Earl Gray?

Broken-hearted lovers
Weeping endlessly,
At some point will succumb
To a nice cup of tea.

In any crisis you can name
When you are shocked and wobbly,
You will be as right as rain
After a nice cup of tea.

At any celebration too
Excited and happy
To pick you up and calm you down
A nice cup of tea.

The wise old sage he nodded
Kind of thoughtfully
'Great men through countless lifetimes
Disciples of philosophy
Have searched in vain for the answer
To this ancient, most profound of mysteries.

For centuries I myself have pondered
And it never occurred to me
That the answer to everything
Was a nice cup of tea.'

He smiled a wry smile
And walked into the light,
I had a sneaky feeling
He did not think I was right.

He turned once more and looked at me
A look most deep and long,
'No, your answer is not right
But it also is not wrong!'

And he left me with this puzzle
Of eternity,
There was only one thing for it
A nice cup of tea.

And as I drank this nectar
A bolt came from above,
Of course the answer is only right
If the tea is made with love!

Lynda Hughes

Firework Display

The day was fine, hardly a cloud in the sky
Children dressed up, this well-clad guy
With a scarf round his neck, a hole in his hat
Nobody noticed the error, as people did chat.

'A penny for the guy,' the children did proclaim
'Well,' said one person, 'can you explain?'
A child said, 'Really, we want to set him alight'
An innocent person said, 'Well, he looks alright.'

The person, 'Why bother, he looks well dressed.'
'Again,' said the innocent, 'I am impressed.'
'Can't you see he is just a guy?' said a child
'Why bother to burn him?' The person was mild.

'It's firework night,' the child said. 'Can't you please give money?
Another person gave him two pounds, 'Now, we are in a hurry.'
The children thanked her, 'But we haven't enough for a rocket!'
Another person gave them more out of his pocket.

'Thank you,' said the lads, 'now we are on our way'
As it was getting dark away from a nice day.
'Shall we really burn this guy?' a child had a doubt.
'Of course, said one, this is what it's about.'

So off they went with the Guy, homeward bound
Buying fireworks on their way, lighting a bonfire upon the ground.
The fireworks went off, the Guy was burning
With the hat and tie their parents were watching
To see they came to no harm through the lovely display
Upon this cold evening as Jack Frost had his way.

Jean McGovern

Never May These Gospels Scream

Never may these gospels scream
across the purer pages and notes of trees,
whose whispers, now drowned in holy water
could bring His druids to their knees.
Now hush, let me mourn, let me curse in anger
at a clouded baby in a clouded manger.

Never can these poets try
to part the water in my veins
or let my rivers flow with blood
or let faith dine on my remains.
Shatter seven sins let there only be one,
Faith in white lights after the sun.

Together the thoughtless faithful dream,
hands crossed on The Book, over Judas' face,
let their angels and demons run them through,
let my crown of thistles descend them from grace.
Yet blind to my sacrifice these poets drown
on His body and blood until the sun breaks down.

Forever I shall watch and wait,
as His promise breaks and their bones tell lies,
as convention is rooted by thistles and seeds,
as they watch the sun set with mortal eyes.
Aware of my sacrifice these lovers now might
dine on my bread, my wine, and the eternal light.

Andrew Wright

Reunited

(For Sharon Lorraine Young)

I wondered through the years gone by about my little girl,
A lacking feeling, with each day by, my head sometimes a whirl.
At times confused, lost and alone, what if any I should do,
At times behold, life took hold, denied my love for you.

Each day a memory, a chosen moment, with thoughts of you in arms,
Each day a sense of feeling, when I soaked within your charms.
Each moment I remember, when so tiny we did play,
For each warm thought I had of you, I had a better day.

I often wondered endlessly, what had your life become?
Where were you now, who were you with and how your life had gone?
And had you had a moment of wonder there for me,
And did you sometimes feel like I did, like a ship lost out at sea?

The times I sat, I pondered, I thought of times with you,
The times I held you tight in arms, we cuddled like you do.
The times I tucked you in, alas, were all but few,
But memories! Though far and few, I never lost of you.

At last I feel so happy,
My life feels more complete.
My life won't be just memories
When in spring at last we meet!

Raymond Gurney

A Warden's Life

I live in a warden-assisted ground floor flat,
I am given so much food I'm getting quite fat.

Our warden's name is Cheryl and she's really very nice,
She calls to see if we're OK and brings a bowl of rice.

She's always rushing here and there to see what we're about,
We lead her quite a merry dance trying to sneak out.

We put pillows down our beds to pretend we are asleep,
One of us acts as a decoy as off the others creep.

I know that we are naughty but we're having so much fun,
To keep our dear poor Cheryl working at such a run.

'Help Cheryl, we have lost our keys, oh help us Cheryl please,
We can't get in to have our dinner; we're having pie and peas.'

We're going off to the bingo hall or so we all had thought,
But most of everyone's planning had really come to nought.

Cheryl's tied all our Zimmer frames together you see,
Thinking, *that will teach them to put one over on me!*

Our Cheryl's going home now; she cannot keep from yawning,
'I'll see you all again,' she says, 'but not till Monday morning.'

Olive White

The Travelling Tramps Visit Spain

Hannam and Hamps in Madrid,
On holiday, here's what they did,
At the airport they landed with a wave and a smile
Then on to the Metro they swaggered in style.
Hamps had his trombone ready to play,
Hannam was strumming his guitar on the way.
After thirteen kilometres pulling luggage along
They had collected ten euro for playing their song.
It was quite a cute number with the notes upside down
The key was unusual and caused the Spanish to frown.
'I just understand it,' said Hamps with a grin,
'The notes we are playing have our message within.'
'Try a blue note with bubbles,' was Hannam's reply
Hamps just slid the new blue note way up into sky.
A new kind of sound resulted within
Madrid just fell silent at the Hamp's Hannam din.
At their Carlton Hotel's reception desk,
They took a musical break by deciding to rest.
The hotel staff began to shiver with fright
As the pair signed in with their smile of delight.
The room they were given was on the top floor,
A twin-bedded en-suite, number six hundred and four.
The lift was quite tiny with no room to move
But they still tried to continue to get into the groove.
Hamps trombone notes rattled the door
Backed by Hannam's guitar as they mounted each floor.
Vibrations completed the lift came to a stop
And with luggage they entered their room at the top.
Hamps shouted with glee with a Spanish ole
Hannam unpacked the vodka to liven their stay!

Ernest Hannam

An Ode To A Dying Village

'Oh no!' You exclaim when you first hear
A block of flats going up so near.
One metre from your boundary line
And about the size, you must not whine.

The council gives the go-ahead
Although you've told them all you dread
The noise, the dust and the bonfire smokes
To clear the site for the builder blokes.

All summer long, up they go
These flats that the council did not know
Would upset the village and its lovely scene
If they lived here, would they be so mean?

People come here for a village life
Away from the flats, noise, stress and strife.
But now a can of worms is open
More flats may appear cos the council's spoken.

They'll argue the point we must build more homes
For the young and the needy but can they get loans?
Most of them want an affordable place
To rent or to buy at a price they can face.

The developers rub their hands with glee
As they forward their plans with the appropriate fee.
They'll argue their point and to the villagers fear
'Oh no!' They exclaim when they first hear.

Kathy B

Quote The Raven

In dark times we've seen the cultural glow,
the masterpiece of Burns and Poe.
The way their words did tell a tale,
many have tried and many have failed.

Black is the bird, some say messenger of death
with contempt in his eyes, the freezing of breath.
The raven's sign, a thing of the mind,
into your darkest depths, you struggle to find.

A master of darkness, Poe carved in blood,
as black as the night in eerie woods.
The house of the dead, the spirits to call,
the raven's the sign, the shadows of tall.

Beware the signs that behold your faith,
black feathers at night, eyes full of hate.
The passion of life, the spirits to soar,
through Poe's eyes and yours, we quote never more.

Patrick Mullen

Mouse

Pitter-patter of tiny feet
Across the darkened floors they quietly creep
Looking for crumbs from the meal before
Ducking down they pass under the door

Little eyes that see through the night
Small sharp teeth into food will bite
Hair so fine, almost like silk
They stop to lick on some drops of milk

Making their way back to the den
When all is quiet they will try again
In their bed huddled up like a ball
Happy for the crumbs found on the floor.

Christopher Cloarec-Pollard

Copy Cat Syndrome

Must get your peace of mind into their being,
With watchful envy they are all-seeing.
Quickly befriend, for they'd like to be you,
To possess many acquisitions that you do.

You've come a long way, they cannot compete,
Some frustration they aren't able to beat.
The situation beyond recall gets under their skin
Need to retaliate, soon enmity will begin.

They can never be you, never be the same,
Will malign, ridicule, activate your name.
It is all they can do, they cannot resist,
With no need of them, you can peaceably exist.

Betty Bukall

Wet Day

The rain played music on my hat
Into my face it softly spat
I do not think it meant to be rude
I was just pleased I was not nude!

A bird stood still enjoying the shower
Rejoicing in its cleansing power
The flowers nodded and nudged each other
Knowing each would grow tall as her brother

Then home I went with my wet, limp labs
Until on the tarmac the circled pools
Had us dancing around
Like silly circus fools.

Barbara Tozer

At Seventy-Six

At seventy-six I have a wheeze
No, not the one that demands more breeze

At seventy-six, I have some moans
No, not the ones from my painful groans

At seventy-six, I am in a wonder
For I think of the here and the yonder

At seventy-six I look back in amazement
At life and all its changement

From modest upbringing, but a very good school
In surroundings where some may lack even a stool

To the jungles of Africa and all its excitement
Having come from a big city with a history of enlightenment

At seventy-six I do my garden
But the demolition expert brooks no pardon
A few fake flowers and concrete divine
Green is rubbish and who needs a vine?
Its cut, remove, prune and uproot
But wait a minute! Don't we want nature's colourful suit?

A garden takes years to nurse and prepare
But with hoe, spade, shears we can end in despair

Now, don't go on about all this
Start again and all will be bliss

At seventy-six I've seen many a change
Some expected but some were strange

I've seen the people of my country
Kind, courteous but sometimes sultry
Many a rural setting, possessing of a donkey
But mostly they can only boast some poultry

The elite and the educated were a joy to know
And worthy of every good relationship to sow
Suave, well dressed, sometimes tarboushed
Eloquent, good humoured with prejudice untouched

We had the Greeks, the Italians, the French
The Armenians, the Turks and the British entrenched
We spoke all their languages as children we played
In schools and the holidays, but our Arabic never swayed

We loved to learn from them, and they also learned our ways
For they were with us, of us, in all our streets and alleyways

Well, it could not have lasted
For the winds of nationalism really blasted
Blinded by prejudice, and blighted by bigotry
The people gradually ended in misery

At seventy-six, I live with another nation
And visit my country with some trepidation
Never to forget the blessings and privilege
Conferred upon me with generosity and no sacrilege
For I was born and fed and nurtured
Till strong I became and learned and cultured

And lo, I went far and wide to explore
To bring to reality my dreams even to the door
I've seen the Africans, Asians, and Arabs galore
And now I am in Europe where history is lore

The heart is throbbing in London my home
Where respect, education and fellowship is norm

I am proud of belonging to cultures new and old
I have no truck with civilisations growing cold
For one gives unto the other like a tribute to the river
And God, in His wisdom, is the ultimate giver

We need to drink copiously of all that surrounds us
And cherish so fondly our heritage and history with no fuss
We carry it, we feed it, we handle it in trust

For ours is not bigotry, bias or idolatry
Rather a continuum in harmony and sweet oratory.

Nabil M Mustapha

England

I'm glad I've been to England
And seen her many sights,
And had the chance to taste and
Enjoy her sweet delights

I'm glad I've been to England
My eyes are open now
I have our sluggish life and
Our simple wants, I vow.

I'm glad I've been to England
All my surroundings would
I quickly anglicise, and
Re-model as I should.

I'm glad I've been to England
Behold me spick and span
In silk and patent shoes, and
With parasol and fan.

I'm glad I've been to England
And learned to rule my spouse,
For there the wives are bold, and
Command in every house.

I'm glad I've been to England
Where I have learnt to make
Sweet dainty things like tarts and
Blancmange and fairy cake.

Had I not been to England
I'd be at home, all day
Housekeeping with my maids, and
With little time to play.

But now I've been to England
Where ladies oft are out,
I like to call on friends, and
With them, to gad about.

Joana Sam-Avor

Senses

A sky of blue, the golden sun,
The busy bumblebee,
Flowers of all colours are such fun,
These are all the things I love to see.

Listening to the trickle of the stream,
The song of the birds in the air,
In the moonlight, the owl's scream
These are the things I love to hear.

The scent of the hay in the evening,
The bluebells in the dell,
Honeysuckle sweet, and lingering,
These are the things I love to smell.

Blackberries and strawberries growing wild,
Windfalls lying to waste.
All these I gathered as a child,
These are the things I love to taste.

A walk along the country lanes,
Explore the cliff tops too.
And squelching through the gentle rain,
These are the things I love to do.

Soft petals of the roses,
Furry creatures and such,
Babies little pink noses,
These are the things I love to touch.

I sit awhile and contemplate -
And count my blessings too.
For all these things I dedicate
And give my thanks to You.

Betty Prescott

Caged Bird Of Youth

Have you seen a bird in a cage?
Singing, colourful and bright but feeling rage
from her heart locked in the cage.
She may asks herself, is my creator there?
Because beyond the bars there waits an expanse of air
in which she has never soared, as trapped she stays.
Her wings long and beautiful, she cannot spread them here.
She waits patiently as her creator is her only fear.
Will she die before she is able to soar in the sky for evermore?
This beautiful bird has a heart and soul
Or will she live to cry looking out at the sky beyond her reach?

Open the cage, watch her fly
Frightened at first, even shy,
Up she soars - sideways high in the sky,
Swooping and looping and singing on high,
The flock from a distance looks like her,
Wings and feathers, beaks the same,
But nearer still she observes; they ignore her, she goes unheard,
Her colours are bright, purple, green, yellow, blue,
A beautiful bird of creation (not unlike you),
The others are grey, white, black, brown,
Perhaps they come from another town.

Still she searches far and wide
But finds no one like her to fly by her side,
She continues and flies on and on
To search for her kind on another horizon,
As her creator had willed from the day she was born;
Her spirit is soaring,
Her wings are outspread,
Her soul is reborn
As she flies overhead.

Maryam McKenna

If Only . . .

If only . . .
Two small words but of great importance
We use them often
Especially after an unfortunate occurrence.

If only . . .
Separately insignificant words,
Quick to be quoted when another course of action
Could have been followed and made successful.

If only . . .
I could have been more tolerant,
I could have listened,
I could have used my intelligence,
I had stopped to think.

If only . . .
Words generally used in a past tense,
Words to recall regret,
If only antagonists would consult mot confront
And mankind respect the environment.

If only . . .
World leaders would meet and listen to each other
And dictatorial leaders accept democratic principles.

If only . . .
There was more compassion
And we tried to understand others frailties,
Give help to the underdog and defenceless,
Show unfortunates the rightful way.

If only
We could wave a magic wand.

William Stannard

Inequities

I know darkness well, should I dwell
on the inequities of life?
Such gentle lovers finding strife
lustful takers with hurtful souls
politicians and selfish goals.

The poor and weak, too ill to speak
their words are lost amid the wind
the rich, forgiven when they've sinned
hatred is now ubiquitous
the sadness? No one makes a fuss.

Our governments, evil intents
but do they change as empires fall?
Can anyone here, hear love's call
the whispers of the gentle hearts
duplicitous thieves, playing parts.

So what's our role? Who killed and stole
the perfect innocence of Man?
Yet we claim, we do what we can
we pray and preach, the lies we teach
grains on a beach, disabling each.

What's the truth? I'm not a sleuth
but the inequities of life
are causing gentle lover's strife.
Altruistic love battle's rifts
and giving love; Man's greatest gifts.

Des Beirne

Sympathetique

I see the sunrise in your eyes,
watch it set in your hair,
but when I'd kiss you goodnight
you're not there

I laugh with you in the rain
like we hadn't a care,
but when the sun starts to shine
you're not there

Media homing in on the spread
of HIV-AIDS everywhere,
the rhetoric of concern exposed
for an empty chair;
If heaven's kisses bitter-sweet
for the love in our care,
dare we betray, fail to keep it safe
in lust's dark lair?

But for your love in my heart,
I could not bear
to know each time I take a fall
you're not there

Though nature default to creation
or its passion us spare,
come wistful rainbows to the soul,
you are there

Roger N Taber

I Won't Stay And Get In Your Way

I won't stay and get in your way,
I know you've got lots to do.
Just wanted to say old 'Arry passed away
And poor Mary's still got the flu.
How are your corns, are they still hurting bad?
Did you hear about Vera ran off with Nell's dad?
Can't really blame him, his wife was a bag
I won't stay and get in your way.
Hasn't it rained a lot lately, our holiday wasn't much fun
Sid drank too much beer and fell off the pier
Now he can't sit on his bum!
Flo had a go on the machines, won us a nice bit of dough
But in a big hurry, we ate too much curry
And all spent the night on the poe.
I won't stay and get in your way,
I've only a few things to say.
Remember old Bert, he still wears that shirt
It's never been washed to this day,
His wife does no washin' she's too busy noshin'
I won't stay and get in your way.
I've really not asked how you're feeling,
Are you still suffering with piles?
The last time I saw you, just couldn't ignore you
Looked like you'd been out on the tiles.
Anyway, I won't stay and get in your way,
I know you've got lots to do.
It's been so nice to see you but before I now leave you
I really must have a quick poo!

John Wayre

Dad

There is a man whom I call Dad.
I know there are many,
    But that isn't bad
For this one dad, the one I call,
Is better than most,
    No, better than all!

For he is my dad, the one with that laugh,
He creases his eyes up and blurts out a sound,
He cackles a little,
    Then a noise, quite profound;

It gurgles and yelps like a ticklish drain,
Then another big chortle,
    The tears pour, not in vein,
For all of his being is lost in this grin,
So contagiously silly,
    We all must join in.

We cackle and gurgle
    And shout with delight,
Our faces are aching,
    We laugh through the night.

And by the time the morning light comes
We try to remember,
    We try to recall
What was ever so funny that made us laugh so
    At all!

Joanna Wallfisch

The Hard Life

I went to bed last night
Thinking of a new song
And when I woke my heart had sunk
Because she'd gone
And left me all alone.

Time will tell
'Bout the rights and wrongs
Of all the singers
And their songs
And I know now
As I knew then
That mystery has all gone.

When I was young
I went to work,
The wages I earned
Weren't very much
But carried on for my family's sake
For many, many years.

But now,
Oh, now my friend,
I've given up
Nearing the end.

Trying something new,
Entertaining you,
Hoping it brings you
Love and peace.

One day I'll die
And some will cry,
Remembering things I did
That were bad.

I get depressed
And often sad
And all the world
Thinks I'm mad.
Because I was insane
Half my life.

I loved a lot
Of pretty woman,
They were good,
They were friends,
But now,
But now
I can't see them.

Foolish me
Doing stupid things
Learning my lesson
In the prisons
And coming out
With nowhere to live.

All those records
I have bought
And I played them
All the time
And now this,
And now this
Is another one.

Frederick Lewis

Inspiration

When I go to sleep at night
I take with me a twinkling sight
Of a million stars shining bright

They coast on my dreams and make them play
Games of skill and perceptions

Soon to return in impulsive frissons
As starlit stimulators of my ambitions.

Michele Cavannah

Dear Tesco

Dear protestors

We offer you quality in assorted slices.
We offer you competitive reasonable prices.
We offer you employment for your sleepy town.
In accordance with the work plan of Gordon Brown.
We offer you petrol seven days a week,
We offer you the chance to be part of something elite.
Something to shape that desolate place
and change that old factory into a brand new face.
We offer you our fast track twenty more tills,
so you can buy more and spend less on your shopping bills.
Fresh meat, fresh fruit, fresh bread, fresh fish
so under one roof is all you could ever wish
and every day we offer you five new cheap fruit and veg.
'Every little helps' - this is our pledge.

Dear Tesco

How can we teach our kids morals from birth
if you carry on building and raping the Earth?
Yes, you can promise fresh fruit if you please
but how can you provide this without any trees?
And soon you'll have taken over all market stalls
and other shops and reign over all
so we have to worship at the shrine of blue and red
while the farmers turn bankrupt and their cattle end up dead.
So you import cheap meat from abroad down south
and bring over Blue Tongue and Foot and Mouth
and we don't know what's in it as we chew and swallow
and get new illnesses when we wake up tomorrow.
So while you're wearing your manager's tie and shirt
why don't you go promote that every little hurts?
So people let me put this in another dimension,
if you're not annoyed . . . you're not paying attention.

Kerry Moores

The Poppy

The poppy is a sign of eternal sleep
The poppy gives opium, sleep really deep.
How very sad that men have to die,
They shed blood, the colour of the poppy which makes one cry.
In wars and fighting such a waste of life,
Leaving behind such sadness and strife.
The flower is so beautiful with petals soft as silk,
It is a pity such beauty has to wilt.
Yet in its way it symbolises our remembering loved ones
                                        no longer here,
Although in our heart they are always near.

The poppy is a symbol of remembrance and love
The red petals are as red as the blood.
The blood shed by our forces in so many wars,
Please Lord don't let there be war anymore.

Yvonne Chapman

No One Seems To Care!

Homeless people walk the streets in worn out shoes and blistered feet
looking for somewhere to stay so they can sleep the night away.

Under arches you will find them there, as the fire burns they sit
                                        and stare,
sheltered from the wind and rain listening to the midnight train.

The bag lady sits on the seat as the road sweeper sweeps his beat,
people pass here on their way, sometimes she's there night and day.

No one seems to care for these people in despair,
living day by day just trying to find a way
to achieve their hopes and dreams, some selling magazines.

Its time for us to understand and offer them a helping hand,
they all have reasons for being there and sometimes life just is not fair!

Terence Leonard Pilditch

Ode On A Toilet Roll

One of life's unappreciated things
No one considering the comfort it brings.

School children think it's funny
For paper, thrown into the lavatory bowl
And flushed down the dunny
To have the nickname, 'bog roll'.
Even funnier when, after visiting the loo
Someone gets a piece stuck to their shoe
Which they trail for hours round the school.
They feel such a fool
(When eventually discovered).

Students throw it out of first floor windows
To decorate the trees below.
(They stare in horror at the empty holder -
Their bum cheeks growing ever colder
On the freezing white seat -
Praying for just one soft sheet
To be secretly stashed away.
Alas! It isn't their day!)

Presenters on Blue Peter encouraging children
To waste the paper to get to the roll inside -
A measure most drastic
(With obscene amounts of sticky-back plastic)
For a 'Here's one I made earlier'

I for one just feel forever thankful
That 'tracing paper' is no more
And that old read-from-cover-to-cover newspapers
Are no longer shoved under the door,
To be turned from being 'read' to being brown
And be flushed straight down.

Toilet roll is very humble -
It never complains about work conditions:
It has no inhibitions.

Always soft, strong and very, very long
Shame it does nothing to absorb the pong!

Lauren Hesford

Treasured Memories

Memories are precious
They are the treasures of time,
You can collect all of your years
If your memory is fine.
We spend all our life
Building a past,
Storing and filing
In our memory, to last.

If your eyesight should fail
There are aids we can get,
We can read books in Braille
But we must never forget.
With walking and hearing
We can always get help,
There are wheelchairs with steering
And you can hand sign yourself.

If we become old and frail
We are never condemned,
When our memory has failed
There is nothing to mend.
With all of these problems
And age we can cope,
But with no memory at all
There's no life and no hope.

Dianne Audrey Daniels

National Service

With so much affecting our daily lives at present
The idea of supplementing our armed forces is an event,
Our young people of today need help anyway,
Their training with fitness would be a good way.

In the past our country has set an example
With so many volunteering numbers were ample.
However, we live in a changed world of evil,
This has led to necessary forces that are not fearful.

Many will say it's costly, but at least a solution,
As one would expect the government needs a motion.
The important use of manpower is primary,
From early days we have relied on voluntary.

There is no doubt with youngsters misdirected
The chance to improve is really recommended.
We have pride with our forces seem,
Therefore we should seek fame together.

So how will we get the government to intervene?
There needs to be pressure on scene.
Perhaps a letter in the local press
Might register with the public and impress.

William Burkitt

I Have To Make A Lie

As I walked my brother to the door
And said to him, 'Good luck at university and goodbye'
A naughty tear runs down my face
And I noticed that I had begun to cry.

My brother asked me, 'What happened?
Why are you crying?' he said.
'I have got terrible hay fever,
That's why my eyes are watery and red.'

I took my sister to the airport
I said, 'Have a great holiday and I will miss you.'
Then a tear fell down my face,
It was completely out of the blue.

My sister asked me what was wrong,
Why I had begun to cry?
I answered back,
'I have put my finger in my eye!'

Sometimes I cannot control my tears
And sometimes they made me feel really shy.
So every time my tear comes out
I have to make a lie.

Marinela Reka

Noises In The Night

I woke up from my sleep one night
And heard an awful crash,
My heart was racing really fast
As I listened to each smash.

I thought it maybe was a burglar,
I was so scared that I froze,
I lay in silence listening
Snuggled up under the bedclothes.

Then finally I'd had enough,
I couldn't wonder anymore,
So bravely in the dreaded dark,
I crept across my bedroom floor.

I slowly peeled back the curtains
And dared to take a peek,
My body shook with terror,
I knew I couldn't speak.

My eyes scanned around the misty garden
As I searched for what could make such a din,
When suddenly it happened
A *bang* came from the bin!

I dropped the curtains in a flash
And fell down on the floor,
The moonlight shimmered on my face
As if to say come see some more.

But now I felt so wide awake
There was no way I could sleep,
So I tiptoed down the creaky stairs,
To have another peep.

I gasped as I reached the kitchen
With the icy cold tiles on my feet,
The door was getting closer
What was it I would meet?

My shivering hands reached out
And turned the rusting key,
My heart was beating faster,
I was afraid of what I'd see.

I slowly pulled back the squeaky door
And thought I'd take a chance,
So I stepped out into the cold air
To try and get a glance.

I couldn't see or hear a thing
And I began to yawn,
The frost danced in the moonlight
Like sparkly diamonds on the lawn.

I thought I'd sit for a little while
To see if daylight would soon come,
When quickly I began to yell
I felt prickles on my bum!

I jumped to my feet so startled
And there sitting in the fog,
With peering eyes and a spiky back
Was a freezing cute baby hedgehog!

He had managed to climb into the bin
And he had sure made a big mess,
Bu the poor little thing was so cold
And searching for food I would guess.

The moonlight was starting to fade
And another day was about to appear,
So I ran upstairs to my parents
To tell them guess what is here!

I begged Mum and Dad and I pleaded,
'Could we keep the hedgehog as a pet?'
But they sadly said, 'No he needs care'
So we had to take him to the vet.

The vet said they'd find him shelter
And it wouldn't take very long,
The winter soon would be over
And he would be outside and feeling strong.

I nicknamed the little hedgehog Harry
I won't forget how he gave me a fight,
When I woke up from my sleep
With a strange banging noise in the night.

Amy Owens

The Snowman

Shrieking with laughter
Having a ball,
Way up above
Snowflakes still fall.
First build his body
Add on his head,
Next comes his scarf
Striped blue and red.
Put on some buttons
Then add his face,
To finish him off
Put a big hat in place.
Keep in your memory
Him standing so strong,
For when the sun comes
He soon will be gone!

Wendy Orlando

My Flower

Little smiling pansies
Swaying in the breeze.
Have you any time for me
So nice beneath the trees.

Everyone so different
So human and so nice.
Nodding heads and budding flowers,
All coloured and so bright.

Shall I pick them one by one?
So different and alive.
For soon their colours and their smiles
Will make the house more bright.

Madeline Richardson

The Pain

The pain of sobriety
Is the stain of regret
And when you remember
You'd rather forget.
The warmth and kindness
You once shared
Are now just memories
Distorted and blurred.
Give it time is what I'm told
Open your mind
Let it go.
Think of a time, think of a place
Someone special
A comforting face.
Every day this murderous fight
The fear and coldness
Approaching the night.
But how can I stay away
From the madness
Keeping me sane.

Jonathan Doran

Diffuse Your Muse!

Publish your book now with Proprint
With Proprint now publish your book
Start writing with zest
Get it all off your chest
You'll know when it's finished
It's all for the best.
Be it poetry, true life or fiction
Or ninety-one ways how to cook
Just publish your book now with Proprint
With Proprint now publish your book!

G Baker

The Party

I'm eight today! Today I'm eight!
I'm standing by the garden gate.
The sun is bright, the day is hot,
I feel so good and you know what

My friends are coming to my home,
Everyone I like will come.
We'll have a party, lots of treats
And games and prizes, lots of sweets.

And if the weather isn't cool
We can swim in the swimming pool.
I expect we'll make a lot of noise
But we're just little girls and boys.

Oh what fun it's going to be
When I see the gifts they're bringing me.
Though Mummy says I shouldn't say
That's what I'm thinking of this day.

I think I heard a running sound
They're at the corner, running round.
Yes, they're all here, no one is late,
This day so special because I'm eight!

Gillian Petainek

The Silly, Funny, Rascal Clown

The doorbell rings and off Mum runs
To see what that could be,
The silly, funny, rascal clown
Jumps in and points at me.

'Now birthday boy, I know it's you
I can see it in your eyes.'
The silly, funny, rascal clown
Pulls out a big surprise.

A birthday gift, a birthday gift
My first one of the day!
The silly, funny, rascal clown
Has brought me games to play.

All day long was joy and laughs
And gifts galore for me
The silly, funny, rascal clown
Has brought a cake for tea.

Now the bestest gift he saves till last
Though it made my mum go mad,
The silly, funny, rascal clown
Turned out to be my dad!

Jamie Parkinson

Yorkshire Discovery Tour

Roman soldiers made Ermine Street
So London York trips were made fleet.
Dick Turpin created some mayhem
And it became the A1 (M).
Then Robert our guide safely drove
Woods' bold tourist wanting to rove
To discover Yorkshire's splendour
And Aldwark Manor's provender.

It is not what Yorkshire first reveals
That excites, but what's concealed
For her true lovers to explore
Of heather moors, dales, towns, seashore,
Heartbeat and Herriott film set lore,
Stately homes, steam trains and much more.
So thanks Robert for those fine sights
And hotel for good meals and nights.

Ronald Rodger Caseby

Summer

I love the summer shades of green
In the woodlands I have been.
Roses golden, pink and red
Old creaky gates, the garden shed.
Sandy endless beaches
Where sky and sea meet shore,
Cragged rocky features
Of cliffs formed long before.
Days stay memorable and long
Blackbirds light our way with song.
Summer, summer, bring us back
All the warmth and joy we lack.
To recapture that magic time
When we were kings of rhythm and rhyme.

Nigel Evans

You Are The . . .

Dazzling rays from a dewdrop
Divine smell from my coffee cup
Puzzling patterns in my trinket
Pine leaves of my pot plant, uncut
Sizzling sound of sausages
Signed schedules for voyages
Glimmering disc of flames in the sky
Golden glory of this midday
Simmering drops in an estuary
Wooden pillars of this green canopy
Shimmering dunes of a beach in noon
Garden scent of this street in June
Crinkled clouds of this twilight
Brilliant beam of my lamplight
Sprinkled stars in the sky, lucent
Radiant smile of a fresh crescent
Wrinkled dreams shed on my pillow
Pleasant tune floating from the radio.

Nasheeha Nasrudeen

Unstoppable

Walking home from school is something I hate
They have already determined my fate
My legs turn to jelly and there's sweat upon my head
I try to run home, home to the safety of my bed
But then a hand clutched at my bag
And I know what it is and my whole body sags
There's no one around no one to help
So no one hears my painful yelp
I'm swung around and turned to face
The pack of monsters I'd tried to race
The insults hurl right over my head
And the slaps turn my cheeks a bright red
There's nothing I can do, nothing I can say
I guess things will just have to carry on this way.

Joanna Frankwick

Words Entwine

The sea of words
Swirl around,
For in it you will find,
Magical mysteries combine.

Its currents or moods
Sway this way and that
Causing power and strength,
Determination with no tact!

Then a tranquil flow
Soothing and gentle,
Into rapids and rage,
Completely mental!

Dark and mysterious depths
Scary but tempted
Creating achievements to a goal
Sensational or demented.

On the crest of a wave
As all flows in time,
Clear water and harmony, where,
Water, life, words entwine!

Ann Beard

The Buzzards

The buzzards are sun-high,
he and she, tracking,
sliding, slipping, tacking.

They mind us not at all,
he and she, proud,
disdainful, against the cloud.

The bond crow-broken, they flee,
he and she, far-eyed,
far-seeking, feather-wide.

Retreat has dignity, style,
he and she, resigned,
patient, leave them behind.

Then tumbledown, like twigs,
he and she, falling,
wings a-tangle, near stalling.

They regain level flight,
he and she, and lazily they
scorn us out of sight.

David Green

War

The hour approaches, meant for detention
A sigh from those looking for ascension
Business affairs and issues relent
Curious minds follow the bitter scent

Eager hand stretches to scratch
To open the gate and find a way to detach
The new life seems much like a game
A camera capturing life in a single frame

Desert sands seek rain for lubrication
Criminal minds seek psychology for exoneration
The earth has detected poison in her soil
The olive trees are burnt, there is no more oil

All has changed, we need a new map
Genetics have created flowers without sap
Soldiers in the trenches hide from the shells
Deaf to the never-ending ring of church bells.

Emily Petrolekas

Our Meeting Place

Reflections of the past my mind doth fill;
the dept of pain no one can ever see.
Immersed, my heart is lost to waters still,
where dark despair doth now take hold of me.

This place I dwell cares not for love; long lost,
nor offers me a kindly guiding hand.
For what I had has gone and at my cost
my cruel fate I see now, life had planned.

Could love return, or is it all too late?
All ears are deaf, it seems, to my last prayer.
What choice is there? Now I must sit and wait
till Death's cold fingers grasp and take me there.
Without my love, then death makes me complete.
This place, no more a place where we shall meet.

Pat Little

Maj Waghorn's Statue At Chatham

Here the stalwart hero
this man of bygone years
upon marble plinth you gesture
'I suppose' to remind the likes of modern man
the conquests England's shown.
His battles great bloody victories
his fate brave, it's true,
but not of marble are ordinary men
the likes of I or you.
Then here stand you in marble
your silent orders clear,
it's pity this vagabond at your feet
your orders cannot hear.
Ah but figure in marble
it's raining now it's true,
but are they raindrops upon your cold cheeks
or do you see him too?

Robert John Collins

Eyes

Two blue eyes to see the world
Windows for me to look through
But I guess it must be night-time
'Cause there's not much of a view.
Yes they sparkle and they shine
Blue as a summer sky.
But what's the use in having two
When I can only use one eye?
Do you stare out of the window
And think of what you're seeing?
Take in the scenery
Notice the individuality of each human being
Or do you look but never see?
You should have my view
Sure, my eyes don't work so well;
But I see so much more than you.

Jaden Whittall

My Beautiful
(Dedicated to my wife and daughter)

My beautiful princess and warrior queen,
being with you both is no longer a dream.
Before I was lonely, empty and sad,
now having you both I'm very happy and glad.

My life is so complete with you both by my side,
God only knows, we are a strong family tribe.
My promise to you is being honest and strong,
from the depths of my heart I will never go wrong.

My love is unconditional, like yours in return,
your smiles are so radiant like the colourful sun.
What a way to spend eternity and life in-between
with two special women, my beautiful princess and warrior queen.

Gavin Manning

A Gift

My love, woo me not with words as so many others have done,
instead, show me your heart through your eyes.
For words can be cheap, when said just for fun
and are too often a cover for lies.

Too many before you have made promises and spoken of love,
whispering words, oh so tender and sweet.
But they were not my true soul mate, my gift from God above,
yet still, they made my fragile heart weep.

You too have been broken, by a love that was not true,
so for you, trust was a thing of the past.
But your natural reserve and suspicion may overcome you,
spoiling the chance of a true love that can last.

So my love, all I will ask of you, forever and today,
will not be demanding or for gestures oh so grand.
I only ask of you, never to hurt or casually throw away,
my heart which I hold out to you in my hands.

Deborah Wainman

The Pavilion Gardens As Viewed By Prinny

One wonders what the prince would make of the scene,
The grounds of his elegant palace supreme.
Thronged with people of every race and hue
Would his royal nose twitch at the scent in the air
When he went to see his lady at her house in the Steine?

As he drove through the gate in a carriage and pair,
Would the lines of traffic cause his horses to shy?
And surely he would wonder at Max Miller's statue there.
The dates on the plaque, 1894-1963
Are something to make him gasp for air.

I think we would agree with Queen Victoria, his niece
Who found Brighton then 'vulgar and mean'.
If today they meant, she would *not be amused*.
And each would say that the changes they saw
Had not improved the garden surroundings in the least.

Anne Furley

Total Recall On The Mountainside Blasket Islands - Co Kerry, Ireland

If we could freeze the movement and stop the path of time
We would all be stuck like statues, no motion there to rhyme.
Everything's a cycle; the hours must tick away,
If only we could stop the frame one moment of that day.
We could all be there together up on the mountainside,
So relaxed, unrestrained - no feelings left to hide.
Would we step back through the window a moment there to play?
We can all recall in memory the uniqueness of that day.
No way to freeze a moment, it's gone and passed on by,
We can never bring back reality no matter how we try.
Friends go on forever; the ties that bind are strong
Always there within us - the memories linger on.

Winifred Curran

A Special Walk

Here in this field the horses run,
Jumping and skipping, they're having fun.
Rolling on their backs, legs in the air,
Looking as if they haven't a care.

As I leave the field some cattle await
By the side of the road at the farm gate.
How lovely they look with their udders full;
From their udders good milk will come.

Across the road a kissing gate stands,
From there I can see the lay of the land.
The path through the field leads to a wood;
What a lovely day, the walk will do me good.

Then along the path I set of to walk;
High above in the sky circles a hawk.
As I reach the wood with its tall trees,
This wonderful place is like a dream.

Once in the wood the sunbeams shine down
What a heavenly place with so little sound.
The path now twists amongst the trees,
The sound of a cuckoo puts me at ease.

Nearing the end of the path a gate I see;
I feel as though the Lord has walked with me
And when through the gate I have passed
This walk with me will forever last.

Passing through the gate, how I love to roam,
Back on the road I make my way home.
On reaching home I sit down to rest,
I'll remember this walk as one of my best.

Francis Allen

Gallowgate, Newcastle

Where the new motorway divides the skeletal
Leazes Football Stadium from cold medieval
walls, there once was bloodstained grass,
and near the graveyard-smelling moorland
a place of bloody butchery, unseen, unmarked
by any memorial. Traffic ribbons tarmac
and only mind-blank street names stare out
at us coldly with nothing to say, undaunted
by white flesh blooded, scaffold and hempen rope,
or by tumbrel of wooden board.
Nothing pierces a gap of cloudy skies
to let sun shafts squeak through,
those carbon copies of Christ crucified
are washed clean, forgotten in Gallowgate:
The stones of St Andrews church are blindfold,
what's left of the old city walls, brain dead.
Nothing here remembers the Catholic martyrs
their absence is like wind among dry leaves,
like rain dimpling old cobblestones with tears,
like mildewed gravestones to alter citizens
indifferent, persistently frigid, wrapped
in unexpected purgatory's shirts of flame,
begging a cool drop of water from the hands
of those dead saints, in Abraham's bosom now
yet smiling down on them who caused such pain.
History's' complex in what it vaguely recalls,
and also in what it has completely forgotten
but the martyrs having passed over are now
bright arrows in the Almighty's golden bow.

Alan C Brown

Wishes He Could Turn Back Time Or Even A Page

He sits alone at the back of the bus
doesn't want to listen to people he can't take the fuss.
Some friends don't want to know him, wouldn't listen to what
                                                              he had to say,
they did not understand him, how was he born that way?
So he sits on his own, who can he talk to on his phone?
Travelling through the city thinks to himself, *town looks so pretty*
then thinks some more, a can rolling around across the floor
stops it with his shoe, he doesn't know what else he can do.
All his life he has played football, nobody ever had a clue
because it wasn't a big deal in his eyes, he never really thought
                                                                    it through
and the ones that didn't know, would they really care?
Now he is lost and confused on the bus upstairs at the back,
                                                feet up against the chair.
Tears building up in his eyes, he's run out of excuses, alibis
                                                          and white lies.
His family understood apart from his brother, come to think of it,
nor did his poor unsuspecting mother.
But they came round and now they are fine, it does take
                                    understanding love and some time.

Life is life; we are who we are, nobody's perfect, nobody by far.
He sits on a bench overlooking the Mersey a lad walks past wearing
                                                          a Liverpool jersey.
He's fourteen maybe even fifteen so much to live for, so much
                                                    he's not seen.
Reminisces to when he was that age, wishes he could turn back
                                              time or even turn back a
page.
Live his life again, without the fear, the tears and the pain.
Walking on eggshells, locking himself away.
Why? Because he was different. Why? Because he was born that way!

Years have passed and all is OK, he met his partner who was
                                              the same way.
Years they have been together standing by each other's side,
                                                there for each other.
A shoulder to lean on when one of them cried.
Times have been rough, emotional hard and sometimes rough
But they have come through it, no more will they run away,
open happy and free, just like life is supposed to be.

Stephen Owen

The Reluctant Footballer

On rain-hazed day years ago
soccer days were a bind
I would usually miss the ball
and fall on my behind.

Deep in puddles I would shirk
praying the ball wouldn't arrive
I would try a lunging tackle
and make a dramatic dive.

The heavy ball weighed a ton
caked with lumps of dirt
and when it struck me on the head
my word it really hurt!

The day I left my senior school
I had a moment of fame
my foot struck the ball sweetly
we scored and won the game!

Alex Branthwaite

The Hidden Secrets Of Her Life

If you don't see her
Will you not see her die?
If you don't love her
Will you not see her cry?
Invisible words that she screams out loud
Her voice so empty, can she ever be proud?

She stares at her friends and she stares at their smiles
Her heart so weak it almost dies
Her stomach so sick of juices and bile
She keeps on pushing that one extra mile.

A screwed up head she thinks
Eternal absence in her mind
Sense, love, stupidity, but nothing links
Nothing can match what she wishes to find.

Her mirror screams out
When she opens her eyes
She's so used to darkness
Her brain reminds
Sitting in the cold
Staring at stars
Dreading the light of oncoming cars.

She fears her school
She hates her life
And nothing can make that old flame relight.

Her parents, her brother, her family and friends
They're all there but then they're not
So alone she sits and screams to stop.

Stop! The green within her eyes
Stop! The blue sorrow from where it lies.
Stop! The pain as she sits alone
Stop the world, that's what it would take for her to go.

Her stubbornness inspires her conscience to grow
The natural beauty proceeds high from low
So occupied she keeps to stop time for thought
But that second that moment catches up to daunt.

Alone she battles to face the world
But alone in bed she rolls up to curl
Into a ball to hide from the air
Just as day rushes forth, a nightmare to scare.

Is a nightmare born when good turns to bad?
Does it live when happy turns to sad?
The questions I seek are the unexplained in life
Yet I wait to find a better state of mind .

So I may sit alone in a ball
And I may run that one extra mile
But I shall remember, for I'll never forget
I'm a mere baby stuck in a girl's world.
If you don't see me
You will never see me die
If you don't love me
You will never see me cry.

My invisible words, I scream out loud,
My voice is so empty, I can never be proud.

Shelley Brace

Shells

Never a key for this chest, a heart came second,
Let them laugh for I'm never beckoned,
My reflection never utters a word,
For I'm the sad spirit that's always unheard.
No one can see me, even when the pages aren't lined
Just one look I ask, or maybe they're bound.
Break the lock for I'll show my treasure
And we'll dance with our shells because they won't last forever.

Anthony Orless

Untitled

Is it because I did not choose the right paths or follow
                                                   the roads of roses
or were there never ways all laden with posies?
There is a sadness, pathetic badness which festers and yearns.
I'm burning up in the mundane sequences which entangle,
too much mess to work through, fear to strangle.
Distant nights that echo and moan, scream in the distance
                                                   of that far away home.
Achievement is empty when you cannot feel alive, you try, you fall,
                                                   you bleed and strive.
Time just beats, repeats, over and over, pulls me forward
                                        into the dreams all real and sober.
So much just pushes at my being, suffocating, I am struggling
                                                      to breathe.
The air is rushing, all is screaming I long to grieve,
At my body I stare and remember, it's bound up in shame,
                                               too guilty to surrender.
Too frightened to feel, all chains, enslaved.
My mind is programmed to be plagued, I could weep for freedom,
                                                 a thousand miles.
Yet I'm stuck pretending behind a thousand smiles.
Who wants tears? So hidden this pain, so pathetic to mourn,
                                               agony holds no gain.
This grief unleashed would choke, break, child would rise silent
                                                 she would shake.
I know she died, lost in their arms, frozen in shame, wrapped
                                                     in charms.
She's deep inside where I hide her and lock, I hate her badness,
                                                  I shun and mock.
She took on their dirt, pollution spread with dark deeds,
They entered in, I can hear her pleas.
All closed down, innocence flew, lost, body bound, taken without cost.
No innocent play untarnished or pure deep silences rose taunted,
                                                         dark lure.
No one saw, no one sees, no one saves, child yearns, child weeps,
                                                     child craves.
All these are shunned, 'Do not cry,' they say.
'Do not whisper through your tears or darken this day.

Do not seek some love, some comfort or care.'
Tears were wrong, she died right there.
So who is still alive? I do not know, this person who's sad
                                            and cannot grow,
This being that punishes the child inside, the child who was bad,
                                            that's why they pushed inside.
Was it an excuse, was that punishment real?
I have to cleanse her, I need to feel.
All crashes and turns my insides churn to work yet dark shadows
                                            filter and lurk.
I'm so sick of her disease, someone please take her hand,
                                            I cannot love or understand.
My emotions all mummified, enclosed and bound,
she weeps without voice and speaks without sound.
She dies, loves, leaves, all heaves and grows with the weight,
now nothing is clear, all bent, never straight.
Today I struggle to feel alive, though all breathes and beats,
This badness just destroys as pathos weeps.
Child who never sleeps in silenced slumber, holds fast to fear
                                            as the lies pull her under.
Lay down your beauty as discarded rights tumble,
Fight through the pain as you bleed and stumble.
All time focus in, she escaped her being.
To survive the reality her eyes were seeing,
I will not falter nor fall too hard, cannot let her fail, too much to discard.

Claire Patterson

Intensive Care

Intensive care she told me, an accident you fell.
An operation - resting now. Was this real, could I hear
                                    or was I suddenly in Hell?
No visiting she told me, wait till later on
Just sit at home and hope and pray that in a while you won't be gone.
I couldn't wait, I had to go, in my zombie-driven car,
I don't remember any distance, was it near or far?
The hospital was big and full of faces I couldn't see,
I read the sign, 'Intensive Care' like a magnet pulling me.
I could hardly tell the nurse your name though entrance I had to gain
To see for myself that you were alive, to comfort you in pain.
Uniforms quietly watched and monitored whatever happened there,
The mask, the tubes, the blood, the stitches - nearly too much to bear.
You could talk and hold my hand, everything would be fine,
I could smile and make a joke, while looking for a sign
Of reassurance, of future to come, of normal life once more.
I held back the pain and worry till I got to the door.
I walked along the corridor, my eyes so full of tears,
My head was pounding, my brain seemed numb but oh so full
                                    of thoughts and fears.
I felt so sick, so sad, so cold, so helpless in your hour of need,
I was unable to turn forward the clock so that you would be healed.
I dwelt on the words 'Intensive Care' and prayed that's what
                                    you would receive,
Something for me to hold on to, something in which I could believe.
And although the hours passed slowly and the days dragged
                                    one by one,
I knew when they moved you from ICU, the light at the end
                                    of the tunnel had come.

Angela Hobson

Dieting In Stages

I'm going on a diet soon
To lose some excess fat,
I think I'll start in summertime
Eating salads and things like that

But the days are long, the nights are warm
You're hungry and you're dry,
It's best to wait till autumn comes
Then give it another try

Is September a better time?
The evening chill is there,
The body needs that hot meal now
Followed by a beer.

Just wait until the winter comes
With dark nights and the frost,
It's all too cold to lose some weight
The willpower is all lost.

Christmas now is bearing down
With peanuts and pork pies,
Christmas pud and extra cheese
Make dieting all lies.

Much better to wait till it's spring
The nights are getting longer,
All those Easter eggs are there,
The hunger buds are stronger.

I'm going on a diet soon
To lose some excess fat,
I think I'll start in summertime
Eating salads and things like that.

Frank Harper

I Didn't Know

I didn't know there was a place
where hearts go to when they die,
I didn't now that being a man
meant you are not supposed to cry.

I didn't know how much a loved one
needs to know you care,
I didn't now the pain you'd feel
when one day they're not there.

I didn't know that Heaven was full
of angels we once knew,
I didn't know we're meant to see them
once again one day, did you?

I didn't know to love someone
from the bottom of your heart,
wouldn't stop them from being taken
tearing your life and soul apart.

I didn't know that everything
in life doesn't turn out right ,
and that hearts can still be broken
even if they're loved with all your might.

I didn't know as much as I thought
about how things are meant to be,
especially now there is an empty space
where once you used to be.

I know now!

Christopher Thomas

Dorothy

Angels singing mouths open
Wide with jewels of sound
Crashing, thudding
Their eyes hit the ground
Wings touch my soul
Eclipsed and entwined
What once a half, now seems a whole
Follow me if you must
Dorothy's in Oz I'm guessing
Must have those angels stressing
Just to make me a believer
They found me a golden retriever
Like to catch my bone
Doesn't seem to want to be alone
Memories play like hands on a harp
With each strum a different melody
Projecting picture almost sounded
Winding back, reverse, play
Silence reaches me in uncomfortable glamour
Like a kiss followed by stammer
Heart sounds into an iron hammer
Angels gaze
This is a love craze
Silence surrounding me
Silence surrounding you
Like angels' blanket
Muffled in ears
And in your eyes I see
You play our lives together through the years.

Natalie Williams

Latisha Faye

Fun and laughter and nursery rhymes
With Latisha Faye, they're special times.
Singing, dancing, building bricks,
Full of joy full of tricks.

Big blue eyes and cheeky smile
Says, 'Granddad please, just stop a while.'
She is just the reason why
I realise now what money can't buy.

Cuddles and kisses when we meet
Altogether makes my life complete.
Getting old ain't half so bad
Now that I've become a granddad.

She's just three, sorry, nearly four,
One little girl that I adore.
Got no worries got no strife,
Always happy, full of life.

Latisha Faye, I want you to know,
How much your granddad loves you so.
What on Earth would I just have to do?
It's a new life now that I have with you.

Jeff Hobson

Freedom

An adventure soon to start
Looks impossible to me
The end is as yet out of sight
Just obstacles to see

Journey begins, it's getting tough
I don't think that I'm fit enough
Though once we've ventured through the trees
A will to end appears to ease

'Is that the peak I see ahead?'
But as we near I see instead
A mountain standing tall and proud
'Oh my God!' I cry aloud
Not a task I'd think to do
Its challenge hidden from our view

Now we're here we must go on
Take each step slowly, one by one

Before too long the distance wanes
At last we reach the highest ground
Both will and energy sustain
I marvel at the scene around.

Saffiya Sheikh

Barlborough
(A small tribute)

This wonderful emerald, tranquilising the distressed,
Radiating her solace and on bequest
Peace permeates the impenetrable, soothes the turbulence of mind -
The daily grind.

Equilibrium is returned by the fragrance of spring
Under leafy canopies the feathered sing
The mellow tunes of cuckoo and dove
Turn our minds to kindness and love.

Old coal pits that have long since died
Cragfaced quarries that once supplied
Time-soaked yellow limestone walls
Embellished Elizabethan halls.

Plaintiff waves of goats that are bleating
Whilst sparkling waters add a murmured greeting
To passers-by that linger awhile
To pick posies and repose in style.

Distant sounds in far off grounds
Of cattle lowing, grass mowing, farmers sowing,
Raucous rooks, babbling brooks and muffled bells,
Cries of children playing, donkeys braying, people praying
And running wells.

Giant ash and lime soften gritstone memorials of time
We catch our breath and starry eyed, gaze at bluebell swathes
that hide
The scars of winter's scouring
Amid woods refreshed and flowering.

This whispered paradise - not heavenly bound,
But envelopes aesthetically all around
Ethereal beauty, such treasures we sigh
For this is the Barlborough no money can buy.

André Bradley

A Subtle Departure

Is this what we have become?
You and I so different
And Vastly so
The man coiled in the doorway
Outstretched hand you shun to know

Not content with your material toys
And your wife to eye
Showing you insist
A perpetual parade of worldly goods
What are you proving to me, why persist?

Is it the case of a fallacy great
Grandeur in your thoughts
You feel not
Your lowly beginnings forgotten
Nothing over all others is what you've got

To argue this you naively challenge
Pitch against wizened mind
The void grows
You fail to see beyond tangibility
Onlookers with smirks and raised brows

No more of my mind to you I'll impart
Your greatness is profound
I'm not unkind
You see I know where you're going
And exactly what you'll leave behind.

Oliver Barrett

The Malvern Hills

The great green hills stand majestically
Have been there since creation
Inviting everyone to climb step by step
With views of the countryside,
Views of Herefordshire and Worcestershire
Gardens and fields, roads, churches, houses
Schools and playing fields.
The hills were created by our loving heavenly Father
For mankind to enjoy His creation.
The wild flowers and wildlife
The insects and small creatures
Which thrive on the hills.
My father loved the Malvern Hills
And walked on them many times.
He walked them with his dogs, friends and family,
He loved the air and views.
Praise God for the wonders of His creation
Which we can see as step by step
We climb the beacon of other hills
All part of God's creation.

Jean Martin-Doyle

On Finding Some Old Photographs In The Attic

Oh look! There's one of my mum and dad
Standing near to Southend Pier.
Dad has rolled his trousers up
They look so young and happy my dear
And there's a date in the corner;
It says, August, nineteen twenty-five.
Father had fought in the First World War
And was feeling pleased he'd come out alive.
And just look at Mother in that flappers dress.
It makes me think I want to express
The joy this photo has brought to me.

Sheila Smith

Motherhood

Our golden sons are gone forever
Once the ancient beauty calls,
While life, that swiftly flowing river
Soon in death's dark ocean falls

Drowning all the tears and passion
Spent to rear our darling ones,
Sweeping us in careless fashion
Far from our beloved sons.

Giving life takes but a second,
Sow the seed, the deed is done,
But never can the cost be reckoned -
We must lose all we have won.

Prudence Regan

There Comes A Time

There comes a time when man has to cry
There comes a time when one has to lie.
A time when one is sad
Then comes around pleasure of being glad.
There comes a time when all is well
When all is great, then to educate.
That we must all learn to love and not to hate.
A time comes when we have to say goodbye
Be it life or death, we must adopt courage to get us by.
There comes a time to sit and dream of things that lifts our heart
A time when nature stops and starts so let it be whenever.
There comes a time when life is nigh
Let us all adopt happiness when we say goodbye.

Desmond Chapman

Our Rebecca

She's been seriously ill
But is now doing well
She's so gentle and kind
And wouldn't harm a fly
As she is our Rebecca
Who still needs a kidney transplant
It's so sad to see her ill
And the pain you see in her eyes
Then when it's time to take her pills
She always asks the question why
But she knows they help her to survive
And life is for the living
No matter what the future may be
So she takes her pills to survive
And hopefully they take away her pain
To survive another day
Waiting for a kidney transplant
As she is our Rebecca.

Ella Wright

Changing Room

Changing room so unforgiving
you show off what I've kept hidden.
Too many mirrors at every angle
I can see everything dangle.
Not enough room to swing a cat
let alone all of my fat.
A curtain that is not very wide
any modesty is hard to hide.
So hot in here I can't breathe
nothing fits, empty-handed I leave.

Rachel Mitchell

Flower Died

Family pet, a childhood friend
Warm and cuddly, a natural blend
Of love and warmth to share
Flower was a childhood dream
A welcome part of childhood's scheme
A friend who's always there
Caring, sharing and the things
That loving friendship always brings
Those warming times of pleasure
Alas, this bitter winter day
Little Flower passed away
A memory now to treasure
There's time for mourning, time for tears
To mark poor Flower's happy years
But grief will linger never
Flower's there, she's in your mind
Beyond the tears she's there to find
She'll live with you forever.

Ray Ryan

Spring

Spring is just around the corner
Soon it will be time to plant out the borders
A blaze of colour, a wonder to see
Look after nature and it will look after thee.
Soon birds will be building their nests
And pruning their feathers to look their best.
God gave us all these wonderful things
So appreciate them all which each season brings.

Patricia Milnes

Cannibal King

Mbola, King of Onca Po abides within this fall
The leanest in his hunter tribe, the strongest of them all
With feet as large as pangolins
He tramples monkey beds
In trees so proud
He leaps unbowed
Through rhododendron heads.

His waist is strung with shrunken charms that flounce around and grin
Around his throat are threaded teeth from neck to jutting chin
His hair with vulture feathers blow
And in his palm
The ancient charm
And pride of Onca Po.

His pumice throne is smoother than the flesh of poison toad
Close by all stained where men are maimed, a sacrificial probe
Here, where the loping tigers growl
A woman waits
Anticipates
Her lover on the prowl.

High breasted in her haunt she spoons a sweetened lizard stew
And sometimes poppy pods she stirs with offal in the brew
Then later in Mbola's ears
She softly croons
Unearthly tunes
Embellishing his spears.

Clive Macdonald

Bleak Despair

It doesn't pay to look over at someone on the way home from work.
It is not really worthwhile, those fifteen minutes of travelling together
we make our games of make-believe.

A stolen glance of looking is really not worthwhile,
your tongue is made redundant, no speech required again.
Even you look as well and wonder what is it all about,
we both think I am doing wrong but of course it's something
we will never find out.

I am too afraid to talk because it will come out wrong.
The guy who sits with you, whom I like, I am sure has gotten me wrong.
Is it him I want to talk to? Can you make him see me?
Did you pity me with that gaze the other day when I was trying
                                                      not to look

or did you want to speak with me but ever you dare not really look?
I saw you walk to work today and you stopped and looked and stared.
A secret silent stolen glance, I think to what end will all this lead.
But your kind-faced friend, I call him Ted;
he is the one I missed out the shadow behind you both.
I missed his smile, his glance, a look.
I concentrated on the both of you but ignored poor Ted
                                                  reading his book,
Is he my future? Only time will tell, I will give him a glance, a stare,
                                                               a look.

Darren Morley

Felixstowe Sunset

As the shops closed for the day, a man rode by
with a tray of primroses under his arm, a green-fingered guy.
On the seafront, the calm waves splashed gently onto the rocks,
and the picturesque view of the illuminated docks.

Passing the pier, we stopped near to Charles Manning,
where the fountain cascaded and the amusement arcades
were buzzing.
I bought a large thick ice cream, more like a helter-skelter,
and our son Taylor loved licking into his first fresh wafer.

The smell of fresh chips made us all hungry,
whilst two bikers jumped off the walls casually.
A warm March evening and at high tide,
with stones under the promenade seats after their winter ride.

The clear sky shone with an orange and pink sunset,
as lovers stood on the hill-top kissing as their lips met.
We ended up at Landguard Fort, popular with families having dinner,
lights on inside their car or headlamps shining on the barriers.

Regular ripples and a reflected path to the cranes far away,
waiting no time for a Stena Line ferry to go out, coming back
another day.
It was dark now, only lights on in the cabins or on deck
to recognise the ship's outline, whilst turning your neck.

Adrian Bullard

A Hug's My Drug

Right here and now in this moment in time
I feel a little lost and I'm going out of my mind.
I'm tired and feel trapped in my own skin,
In every bad situation I can't ever win.

I don't want a pill; I don't want no weed,
Right now a hug is just the drug I need.

Deep in my soul, I'm emotionally scarred,
Death seems easy, cos life is just hard.
Obstacles to overcome and mountains to climb,
There's no colour my eyes are going blind.

I don't want a pill; I don't want no weed,
Right now a hug is just the drug I need.

I'm all alone and drowning in my tears,
The pains still there even after all these years.
Whoever said that time can heal the pain
It's not true cos life's a tough game.

I don't want a pill, I don't want no weed,
Will you give me a hug?
Cos that's just the drug I need.

Sarabjit Parmar

Shadow

You keep following me around, watching my every move.
Do you know something that I don't know?
You seem to spring on me when I'm not looking, taking me by surprise.

I believe you're watching over me, making sure that I'm safe.
But where are you when my troubles start boiling over?
You can't be seen. You won't be noticed.

Are you worried when I'm worried and are you down when I can't
face the world anymore?
Mysterious shadow, I want you to be my driving force, my inspiration,
my shield.
But you only protect me when the sun is out and everything is fine.

Martin Dix

Forbidden

Hiding away in corners where no one ever sees
Creeping like little creatures 'neath dark and leafy trees
Holding each other tightly wishing in vain to stay
Loving each other briefly then having to break away
And I want to bring our love out in the sunlight
And shout it to the people passing by
But they wouldn't understand so I simply touch your hand
And only kiss beneath a cloudy sky.

Snatching a little time together a few short minutes from a dreary day
And how those minutes fly while the time apart crawls by
You're no sooner with me than you go away
And how I long to keep you here beside me
And walk hand in hand for all to see
For who are they to say I shouldn't love you
And who to say that you are not for me?
But Heaven up above is witness to our love
And every night I send a prayer to say
'Please break the ties that bind us
One day let the morning find us
In each other's arms and there to stay.'

Ailsa Keen

Didn't We Use To . . . ?

Didn't we use to ride stormy weather
Roll in fields of clover and heather?
And I don't find it funny
That now our glue is runny.
Our bonds just aren't as strong,
Where once our chalk and cheese always got along.
Now it seems our courage is ebbing away
To live, stand and fight for another day.
Do you really think we aren't worth the bother
Like eagles on high that can no longer hover?
Do you think we'll just perish and die
Our strong truth becoming a weak lie?

Sharon Grimer

Peace

As I walk outside
The breeze shakes the leaves off the trees
And carries them all around
Gently lays them on the ground.
I see birds all above
As I think of your true love.

Birds landed on our love-shaped swings
As they lay on their soft wings
Your love they gently bring
As they start their graceful descent.
Delivering a message
God had sent
One thing I know
And will hold so dear
When I see them fly
I know you are near.

Tony Johnson

Blackpool Lights

There's a lot to be said for a weekend away
The sound of laughter, happiness filling the air.
To walk along with the one you love
And gaze at the lights so high above.

The thrill of walking the Golden Mile
This makes a trip to Blackpool so worthwhile.
Excited children everywhere, faces all aglow
Both young and old enjoying this wonderful scene
Seeming happier than they have ever been.
And so all winter through
These memories of a wonderful break will remain with you.

Terri Brant

Just Like Summer Storms

Some stand firm in defiance
Against all prejudice and chance,
Others just pass a kind word,
A kiss, a smile, a dance.

Knights of shining armour
Or poets of pleasing verse,
Actors who can charm a crowd,
A footballer or worse.

Could it be some mentor
Or maybe just a teacher?
Is your hero a high goddess
Or maybe just a preacher?

Some are deadly in battle
And some make peace not war,
Others wear a uniformed strip
And hit the net, they score.

Some heroes' names echo down
Right through the halls of time,
Others may be forgotten about
Before you've read this rhyme.

Some heroes fight for the people,
Others calm a maddening crowd,
Kneel in reverent and silent prayer
Or battles cry out loud.

Of all my heroes, perched at the top,
Is a man who stands out tall,
He's been there from the start
My father, best of all.

His best lesson for me was to make me stand on my own feet -
                                                  independence.

Stuart Adams

The Farmer Takes A Life

The farmer gazed around his land in deepest contemplation
horizon blighted by invaders he had invited with regret.
Would modern times needs be, mask decisions made
for the wind turbines churning to ease the mounting debt.

Thoughts drawn back to when ancestors tilled the virgin land,
contented times though laboured, lovingly devoured.
Heavy tasks simplified by horse and man with nature,
now huge machines vandalising land and hedges scoured.

So he viewed the changing landscape
steady erosion of natures fate,
he could not see the fox the badger
hounded out by tortuous bait.

As he visualised his future facing a computer base,
mountain hills of paper always there before his face.
Knackers yard had an allure - his time had come along,
while the bell tolls for the past, what is life without a song?

Margarette Damsell

Titled

Billy the boxer is fighting again
down at the Palley to defend his reign.
And Harlesden town seems quiet tonight
all on account of Billy's fight.
And Jean works down the Royal,
selling cigarettes at three shillings for her toil.
Pestered all night by a Ted,
she slapped his face, he was told to 'Drop dead!'
And old Ma Maginty has been taken ill,
they say too much gin and the odd pill.
And the motorbike boys roar to the café
they are having a real good laugh.
And in the fish and chip shop, there's a queue,
Mrs Gull gossiping about bad news new.
And the police book young Jimmy for having only one light,
as it comes on the radio, Billy's won the fight.

Francis Page

Our Washing Line

The weather is breezy and plenty of sun
Time to hang out the washing that has just been done.
The clothes are dancing about out on the line
So let's put them to music while I sit and sip wine.

I switch on the iPod and put the headphones on go
And just sit back, relax and enjoy the show.
The trumpets sound and away go the shirts
They are really blowing well and so are the skirts.

The string instruments are next to join in without a fuss
The socks and trousers are strutting their stuff.
Next is the heavy brass, what a wonderful sound
The sheets are flying high and then close to the ground.

In come the guitars and the drums start to beat
The underwear is joining in but being very discrete.
Now the towels and the dusters join in at last
And now all of the orchestra are playing at full blast.

What a wonderful thing the imagination can be
You just have to sit back and enjoy what you see.
Just let your mind wander without any pain
And listen and watch and hope it doesn't rain!

Barrie Butterton

Forward Press Information

We hope you have enjoyed reading this book - and that you will continue to enjoy it in the coming years.

If you like reading and writing poetry drop us a line, or give us a call, and we'll send you a free information pack.

Alternatively if you would like to order further copies of this book or any of our other titles, then please give us a call or log onto our website at
www.forwardpress.co.uk

**Forward Press Ltd. Information
Remus House
Coltsfoot Drive
Peterborough
PE2 9JX
(01733) 898101**